Honor Thy Wife

Honor Thy Wife

A 31-Day Spiritual Journey of Marital Renewal

By Kevin Lowry

Catholic Treehouse, Columbus, Ohio 2025

Honor Thy Wife: A 31-Day Spiritual Journey of Marital Renewal

ISBN 979-8-9924897-0-5

Copyright © 2025 by Kevin Lowry & Catholic Treehouse

Catholic *treehouse*

This work has been prayerfully entrusted
to the patronage of St. Joseph.

Dedicated to Kathi, my beloved and beautiful bride.
May the ripple effects of our marriage endure into eternity.

To our children Christian, T.J., Sarah, Daniel, Maria,
Joseph, David, and Hannah, I love you more than
words can adequately express and hope this book
is a source of encouragement.

And to my parents Douglas and Margaret Lowry,
thank you for providing the best example of a mutually
honoring marriage I've ever seen.

There has been a run of wonderful resources of late offering help to Christians in fostering devotion to Our Lady, St. Joseph and a variety of other saints. Blessed be God! For most people, however, few things can be as practical or life-impacting as growing in devotion to a spouse. This little gem by Kevin Lowry is rich with vulnerable stories, humor, and concrete suggestions that can dramatically impact every marriage. Please read this and give it to every married man you know!

— Fr. John Riccardo
Missionary, ACTS XXIX

Some may wonder why a priest is recommending Kevin Lowry's book on marriage, specifically a book encouraging men to love their wives. The answer is simple: with every marriage I preside over, my prayer is that the husband will love his wife as Christ loves the Church. That's no small task, given that Christ gave His life for His bride.

Kevin Lowry's *Honor Thy Wife* is a heartfelt collection of short, personal stories that offer practical and meaningful encouragement for men to love their wives deeply and faithfully—just as Christ loves the Church. The book is both inspiring and relatable, reminding men of the profound importance of honoring their wives in both good times and bad.

In a culture that often overlooks the beauty of sacrificial love, *Honor Thy Wife* stands as a powerful witness to the transformative power of marriage when husbands truly love their wives in the way God intended.

— Fr. Dave Pivonka T.O.R
President, Franciscan University of Steubenville

God is waiting for you in these pages, and he has a blessing. Even if you're satisfied in your marriage, you'll discover here some way to make it better. God is waiting with nudges or maybe even a wallop. But he won't leave you unchanged when you turn the last page.

— Mike Aquilina
Author, The Fathers of the Church

Kevin offers spiritual wisdom, backed by Holy Scripture, to provide encouragement and practical advice on how to strengthen marriages in a very relatable way by sharing stories and snippets from his own personal life. This beautiful book is a helpful, practical and needed resource in the Church today, I highly recommend it to anyone wishing to cultivate a more holy, healthy and happy marriage!

— Emily Jaminet
Author, Holy Habits from the Sacred Heart

From the words spoken and actions taken by the Lord Jesus at Cana, to Our Lady at Fatima, to countless Popes in Rome, the topic of the family —and in particular the sacrament of marriage—is treasured and defended. In this book by Mr. Kevin Lowry we enter into a practical yet profound approach by which the husband can honor his wife and thus strengthen their marital bonds made rich by their vows. Through Kevin's keen awareness of human nature and his employment of humor one can see how his own self knowledge has grown as a result of his love and honor for his wife Kathi; may it be so for every man who reads this book and then loves the woman who is his wife with honor and respect. As Christ loves the Church may every husband live his wife!"

— Fr. Stash Dailey
Pastor, St. Michael the Archangel, Worthington, Ohio

This is the perfect book for a busy guy who wants to be a better husband. In this easy to read, practical book, Kevin explains how men can step up to be who we are called to be for the sake of our marriage. All married men need this book—their wives will be grateful!

— Michael Hernon
President and co-founder of Messy Family Project

Kevin's approach to directing men on how to honor their wives and live as virtuous husbands is equal parts profound and practical. I found myself nodding in agreement as I turned each page, and I admire the way Kevin shares difficult stories about his own shortcomings to help connect the dots throughout this important guide. Thanks to *Honor Thy Wife*, I've recommitted to some of the most basic building blocks within my own marriage.

— Jeff Schiefelbein
Managing Partner, Undivided Life and co-host of The BeatiDudes

"It's good."

— Kathi Lowry
*super-cute wife of the author and
not an effusive verbal affirmation kind of girl (see Day 22)*

Table of Content

Preface

Better Off Together

Throughout human history, men and women have craved attachment to one another. Even in the Garden of Eden, God himself declared that it wasn't good for man to be alone, so he created Eve. The two of them were better off together.

Since that time, countless people have dedicated incalculable efforts to the same goal: finding a suitable spouse. Now, marriage has undoubtedly taken its hits through our often-poor execution over the course of time. Thankfully, for many people, it's not all toil and drudgery. Throughout history and around the world, marriage and family life have been a tremendous source of joy and fulfillment. We are better off together!

The process of finding a spouse has varied over time and among societies. Just consider the modern phenomenon of people swiping right or left on their mobile phones to find mates! But one aspect of the pursuit has remained the same: we put a *lot* of effort into finding the right person.

However, at the very moment you married your spouse, something mysterious happened that probably went unsaid. That goal of finding the right person was replaced, permanently.

Now you're married, and your new goal is to *be* the right person.

A Consequential Journey

You see, your decision to get married has consequences. Marriage is a calling, a vocation that provides context for the rest of our lives. A marriage that is freely entered into with the correct frame of understanding—that it is to be permanent, faithful, and fruitful—provides an ideal set of circumstances for the spouses and children to flourish. On the flip side, the breakdown of marriage is associated with negative physical, emotional, and financial outcomes for family members, especially children. Either way, the ripple effects of every marriage—including *your* marriage—linger for generations.

The effort you put into your marriage is incredibly worthwhile. Our wives are *worthy* of honor and represent our pathway to a fulfilling life, both now and eternally. You see, marriage is a sacrament of service. We win when we focus on serving our spouses rather than being served. For many husbands, service doesn't come naturally. We might have entered into marriage with the opposite expectation. Maybe we even tried to change our wife's attitude! But eventually, we have to realize that we can only change ourselves. And that's hard, but not impossible.

I hope this book provides the impetus and encouragement for you to take one small step toward honoring your wife and growing in joy and fulfillment. After all, husbands and wives aren't meant to be competitors but rather helpmates with an attitude of mutual love and support. Marriage is a lifelong journey, and it's amazing how even small changes can yield big results.

Renewed And Revitalized

The purpose of this book isn't to give you a step-by-step recipe that will automatically confer perfection on your marriage within a month. Rather, it's designed to offer a few ideas you can pray about and hopefully use. My dad used to give me a standard qualifier for all the perspectives he would share with me: "I'm not the Holy Spirit." I offer the same qualifier, with the same encouragement my dad always gave me: he prayed for me as I'm praying for you.

This project began with a sincere desire to honor my beloved wife better. Kathi and I have been through a lot in over 35 years of marriage. Note that I don't have a Ph.D. after my name. I'm a practitioner, not an expert. Sort of like one of my old adjunct professors in college, I come with real-world experience (including hard-won wisdom from countless mistakes) rather than academic prowess.

I've experienced a rich and blessed marriage with plenty of challenges along the way. Yet I am convinced without a doubt that I'm far better off for having married Kathi all those years ago. We are better off together, and I have faith that by honoring our spouses (with God's grace), the door is open to us becoming saints *along with our spouses*. After all, what else matters?

Let's spend a few minutes together each day for the next month. I'll tell you a few stories, often about things I've done wrong. I hope you'll gain some useful, actionable ideas and perspectives. So let's embark on a journey to renew your marriage, to strengthen it and bring it increased blessings and graces.

Your wife is worth it, your marriage is worth it, and your transformation into *being the right person for your wife* is within your grasp.

Introduction

When I told my wife that I wanted to write this book, she laughed.

To be fair, it wasn't a scornful laugh. It was more of a "Dude, you haven't always done the greatest job in that area yourself," laugh of wry amusement. I didn't quite catch if there was an eye roll to go along with it.

Of course, she's right. I haven't always been the best husband. I became aware of the need to do a better job of honoring my wife early in our marriage, with an incident that was a jarring eye-opener for me.

Kathi and I were at the Christmas party for my CPA firm. We had been married for a little over a year and managed to score a babysitter for our infant son. Date nights were rare back then, with extended family living hours away and us living on an excruciatingly tight budget.

This was my first professional job out of college, and I was a bundle of nerves. As a member of the newest class of staff accountants, I was intent on creating a positive impression. Many of my colleagues were from more prestigious universities than mine, had multiple offers from large CPA firms upon graduation, and seemed super smart in a vaguely intimidating way. On the other hand, I had managed to squeak my way into the firm right at the end of the recruiting season. It was no secret that the firm had an "up or out" policy, so either we were progressing in our careers or... not. The firm made cuts every six months at the staff level where I was, firing those they didn't think could cut it. As a result, we were all coworkers and somewhat wary competitors at the same time.

That night, I hoped to impress my colleagues and, even more so, the all-important higher-ups in the firm who held my fledgling career in their hands. I had a family to provide for and was struggling to adjust to the rigors of public accounting. My angst was palpable.

What transpired that night is a bit of a blur. Attempting to be witty, I told a couple of jokes in a small group setting at my wife's expense. I still remember the hurt look on Kathi's face. Immediately, I had a sinking feeling that I had screwed up.

Tim, a senior manager in the firm, yanked my arm–*hard*. His pull on my arm didn't have the feel of being an optional request. Taking me aside he said, "Hey, I don't know what you think you're doing, but you need to stop it, *now*. Do you hear yourself? You're being a complete jerk, and talking about your wife that way lacks class. It's embarrassing! Don't you call yourself a Christian?"

In an instant, it was as if I was an onlooker to the scene, absorbing the group's emotions. A colleague and his wife glanced awkwardly at the floor in distressed silence. Tim's piercing glare was indignant and fiery. Kathi stood in bewildered, pained sadness. Regret and shame suddenly welled up within me. How could I have been so stupid?

I had wounded my precious wife by allowing my foolish pride to get the best of me. My immaturity was on full display to my colleagues. Tim was not just an important higher-up in the firm but also a guy I deeply respected, and I had provoked him into delivering a scalding rebuke. Humiliated and red-faced, I stumbled through an apology and glanced at Kathi. The hurt in her eyes only intensified my regret. The love of my life didn't deserve to be treated like that.

The entire event left a mark on me, and to this day, remembering that evening makes me shudder. Yet I learned a valuable lesson that night: I need to honor my wife better.

In the years since that fateful night, I've devoted myself to doing exactly that. Let me state up front that I haven't always been successful. I've made plenty of mistakes, and there have been many peaks and valleys along the way. But through the journey, I have gotten better (independently verified by Kathi), and the effort has been incredibly worth it!

You see, I'm crazy about my wife. Crazy! She is an absolutely amazing, incredible woman. We've been married for over 35 years, and my attraction to her is every bit as intense as when we first met. My love for her has grown, strengthened, and deepened. We have eight children, (now adults,) and a burgeoning gaggle of nine grandchildren. We have experienced profound struggles and triumphant joys, tear-inducing heartbreaks and quiet contentment.

It has been a truly epic love story.

I'll bet you've got an epic love story of your own. I'm also willing to bet you've made a few mistakes along the way too, but I am confident that you want to be a good husband. Otherwise, why read this book? You probably want your wife to flourish, but how to help that happen might not be intuitive. Let's face it, guys. At some level, the woman you married is a puzzle.

To complicate matters, we're living in a culture that isn't always supportive of us honoring our wives. When was the last time you were part of a group of guys speaking positively about their wives? In the office? The gym? Or worse, the locker room? Do you see men speaking positively about their wives on television or hear it on your favorite podcast? Not so much. Unfortunately, many husbands today have become mired in our culture's downfalls. Challenges abound, including porn, infidelity, rampant divorce, loneliness and distraction. Some days, the headwinds can feel more like a hurricane.

So why write this book? After all, as I mentioned before, I'm a regular guy who has made more than his share of mistakes along the way. It's simple, really: I'd like to share a few stories about a regular guy who loves his wife and has become a better husband since that fateful night over 30 years ago when a grave mistake became the impetus for change. I want to challenge and encourage you to be a better spouse, too. If I can do it, so can you!

Even with our imperfect efforts, I'm convinced that a ripple effect goes well beyond our own marriages. We'll impact other souls, including those we co-create. I'm a true believer that small changes—along with grace—can yield big results. Our faith provides the antidote to the challenges we face. By honoring our spouses, we can help them truly flourish while also finding joy and fulfillment ourselves.

Together, let's say a prayer for our wives. Then get comfortable, grab a coffee, and let me tell you a few stories. I'm grateful to be your companion for the next month or so, and I hope to provide you with some practical—yet achievable—challenges. Honoring your wife and being a better husband *is* possible. By starting this book, you've taken the first step on an extremely rewarding journey.

Ready? Let's get started...

Remember

How sweet is your love, my sister, my bride! how much better is your love than wine, and the fragrance of your oils than any spice!
— SONG OF SOLOMON 4:10 —

The first time I saw Kathi was in college. From the other side of a crowded room, I remember the toss of her blond hair, delicate feminine form, and radiant smile as she talked and joked with friends. I was utterly transfixed. *Wow!* I remember thinking. *She's beautiful!* My life's mission became clear in an instant. I needed to meet her, win her, and grow old with her.

When we were dating, I remember being completely absorbed by her beauty. Spending time with Kathi, talking with her, being mesmerized by her sparkling blue eyes, and just being in her presence was intoxicating. My dear late mother-in-law observed that we seemed a bit infatuated at the time. This was completely true (at least on my part), and it remains so to this day.

Part of falling in love with Kathi was coming to recognize her gifts, which differ so much from mine. I majored in accounting in college while Kathi studied nursing. I've long appreciated her practical caring for others, which comes so naturally to her. That's not the way I'm wired, but her strengths and positive qualities blow me away. I think of them as her superpowers.

These superpowers have been on full display throughout our marriage. They have been tested and strengthened during the 35 years we've been together. When our kids were little, Kathi was the heart of our home. As our family grew larger and the kids grew up, she managed everything from minor daily dramas to bigger challenges, including one child with medical vulnerabilities and another who struggled with addiction.

More recently, when my mother-in-law was diagnosed with brain cancer, Kathi bravely fought to care for her until her passing, while still being the heart of our home. This was on the heels of one of our sons battling lymphoma and another recovering from a complex GI surgery. The emotional weight of these trials was enormous, yet my blue-eyed beauty rose to the occasion and cared for our family through it all.

What first attracted you to your spouse? When you fell in love, what about her resonated? Often, a physical attraction initially elicits our interest, but there's more to her than that. What was it about her character, her personality, and her intellect, that endures? What were her superpowers that you admired?

Mindset

It's so easy to be distracted by discontent. Take time to reflect today on the qualities that initially attracted you to your spouse. Think about those qualities and some of the good times you spent together as you fell in love with her.

Action Item

Though I'm sure there are many, identify just one of your spouse's superpowers you have appreciated about her since you first met, and tell her about it.

Pray

Pray constantly, give thanks in all circumstances;
for this is the will of God in Christ Jesus for you.
— 1 Thessalonians 5:17-18 —

Kathi and I only have one teenage daughter at home now. As with many teens, Hannah has perfected the gift of embarrassing her parents. I suppose it's good for our humility.

One such embarrassment happened while we were walking out of Mass one day. We happily greeted a priest much beloved by our family, Fr. Stash Dailey. Hannah had recently returned from the local Catholic Youth Summer Camp held by Damascus,* and while there she had experienced intense joy in Eucharistic adoration. Rapturously describing the week's events to Fr. Stash, her elation suddenly trailed off. "My parents don't take me to adoration, though," she said wistfully.

Shocked and wide-eyed, Kathi and I looked at each other. Hannah was right.

---

* A terrific organization! Visit them at www.damascus.net

Hannah's adoration deficit has since been rectified, but it reinforced something I've long believed: Prayer is central to the Christian's walk and the vocation of marriage.

Part of my job as Kathi's husband is to help her get to heaven and help both of us grow in holiness and charity. What's the most powerful way to do that? *Relentless* prayer.

How is your prayer life? It's an important question! Having a plan for this area of your life is essential. Prayer for your wife is one of the most important elements of a good marriage.

Here's one approach that I like because it's simple and memorable. I remember reading this in one of the books by the late Fr. Michael Scanlan, President of Franciscan University for many years. It's based on the acronym ACTS:

A: Adoration *(giving God the glory for who he is)*
C: Contrition *(being sorry and desiring to change in the future)*
T: Thanksgiving *(being thankful for your wife, even during tough times)*
S: Supplication *(prayers for your wife, her needs, her healing, etc.)*

Remember your wife as you pray through each element. Of course, this isn't the only way to pray for her. Personally, I lean heavily on the Rosary and the Chaplet of Divine Mercy. Offer the graces of the Mass for her. Offer up sacrifices—small and large—for her sanctification. Have Masses said for her. The beauty of our Catholic faith is that there are many ways to pray, and we know our prayers are always heard. No prayer is ever wasted.

Mindset

Given our fallen humanity, our efforts will never reach perfection. However, the graces we receive through prayer help us honor our wives much better than we could ever do alone.

Action Item

Stop everything and say a heartfelt prayer for your wife right now. If you're brave, make a firm resolution to pray for her daily. It can be as simple as "Lord, thank you for my precious wife." However, I'll bet you can do even better than that.

Day 3: Work on Yourself

*Shun immorality. Every other sin which a man commits is outside the body;
but the immoral man sins against his own body.*
— 1 CORINTHIANS 6:18 —

As you probably know, there are seven deadly sins: pride, greed, lust, envy, gluttony, wrath, and sloth.

Are any of them a problem for you? If you're not sure, ask your wife. She knows.

You might identify one of them as what some call a "predominant fault" or area where you seem to struggle. This doesn't mean you're a failure, just human.

Early in our marriage, Kathi and I often bickered or full-on argued over various criticisms we had of one another. We spent an inordinate amount of time attempting to improve each other. It was so easy to see one another's faults.

This has since given way to a greater acceptance of one another's shortcomings and a greater resolve to work on our own shortcomings.

Do you have a problem with arrogance? Hypersensitivity rooted in pride? Gluttony? Anger and a critical spirit? Laziness? What about lust? This last one is among the greatest pandemics ever known to humanity. If you have a problem with pornography, for example, treat it like the destructive forest fire it is and get help.

Identify your most pressing challenge and be clear about the solution required to overcome it. We often dither when making necessary changes in our lives, but we can't let our reluctance keep us in a place of bondage. It's imperative that we're willing to change ourselves to be the husbands our wives need.

As Catholics, we have one of the most powerful means possible to make this happen through the Sacrament of Confession. As a convert, I absolutely love this sacrament. It's still amazing to me that we can approach the priest, who acts *in persona Christi* (in the person of Christ), confess our sins, and then hear—audibly!—that incredible line, "I absolve you from your sins, in the name of the Father, and of the Son, and of the Holy Spirit." It's such an awe-inspiring manifestation of God's love for us.

Beyond absolution, the Sacrament of Confession also provides grace to help us make needed changes. This is *so* important. Guys are not known for asking for help, right? Yet the Lord provides help that takes even our most modest efforts and blesses them.

There aren't any new deadly sins, but we sure have become more efficient in our commission of the old ones. While we're not going to be completely sinless this side of heaven, by committing to working on ourselves every day, we'll grow in grace, virtue, and love for our wives.

Mindset

Remember that part of a good confession includes a firm "purpose of amendment" or intention to avoid sin in the future. When we fall short in our marriage, in areas small or large, we need to be utterly determined to work on ourselves in real and specific ways.

Action Item

Ask your wife, priest, or close friend to help you identify one problem area in your life that you can improve. Resist the temptation to negotiate! Accept what you hear and say, "Thank you." Go to the Sacrament of Confession and ask the Lord for the grace to begin again.

Day 4: Speak to Her with Honor

Above all hold unfailing your love for one another,
since love covers a multitude of sins.
— 1 PETER 4:8 —

Much to my regret, I have not always spoken to my wife with honor. There have been many slip-ups and apologies during our decades together. This is a hard reality since I should know better. I have a fantastic example.

My parents have been married for over 60 years. They're both in their 80s now and struggling with various physical ailments. Dad had a stroke a while back that took his cognition down a few notches. (This is a guy with a Ph.D. from M.I.T.) But one thing hasn't changed: My father is absolutely devoted to my mother and speaks to her with extraordinary love and tenderness. He tells me all the time just how wonderful she is and how blessed they are to be together. It's truly remarkable.

In my 50-something years on this planet, I have heard my dad raise his voice ever so slightly to my mom precisely once.

We were at the cottage in Ontario on a warm summer day. My parents were emptying a canoe, and among the objects getting the heave-ho was a car battery used to power the small electric motor that propelled us to the best fishing spots. With one foot in the canoe and the other on the dock, Mom awkwardly maneuvered the heavy battery. Suddenly, she slipped, and the battery tumbled loudly to the bottom of the canoe. She barely escaped falling backward into the lake.

"Woman!"

That was Dad's sharp response. Of course, he wasn't yelling *at* her. It was clear in the moment that, even with the shot of adrenaline, his concern was for her safety. Dad loves his wife dearly, but that doesn't mean she's incapable of a fleeting moment of clumsiness.

I read an article years ago suggesting that relationships are built up through respect and affection and torn down by contempt. My dad's consistent gift of speaking to my mom with respect and affection—and never with contempt—has created one of the most incredible marriages I've ever witnessed. The consistently loving way Dad has spoken to Mom for the last several decades is not fashionable, but it is possible. If, like me, your track record in this area is—*ahem*—imperfect, you can change that, beginning today.

Our words spring from the heart, so reflect on what's happening in your interior life. Do you take pains to nurture true affection toward your wife, even in the hard times? When Kathi and I argue, we realize that it often results from a loss of perspective. Rather than focusing on the 99% of the person we love and cherish, we focus on the 1% that's harder to appreciate.

Mindset

Before a game, we know that it's important for athletes to "get their heads right" and enter the competition with focus and determination. Are we lazy and careless with our words to our beloved wives? Or do we get our heads in the proper place and recognize that how we speak to our wives makes a big difference in our marriages?

Action Item

If it's not your habit to speak to your wife with honor, start small. Apologize for times past when you have spoken with even a hint of contempt, and make sure you go back to the basics. In your conversations with your wife today, say "please," "thank you," and "I love you" at least once. And don't forget to tell her that you're sorry. Repeat as necessary!

Day 5: Speak About Her with Honor at Work

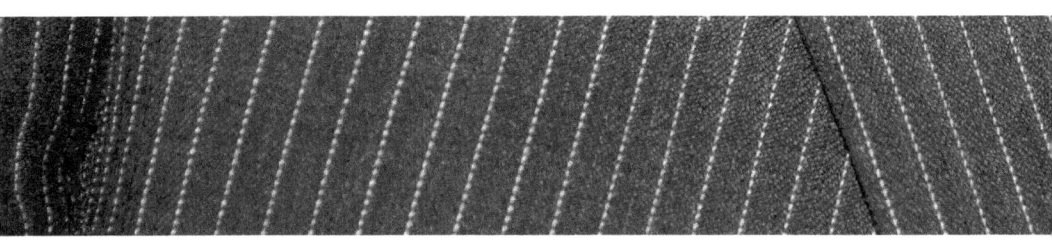

Let no evil talk come out of your mouths, but only such as is good for edifying, as fits the occasion, that it may impart grace to those who hear.
— EPHESIANS 4:29 —

Want to know one of the most powerful evangelization tools available to men today?

Wait for it...

Speak positively about your wife at work.

Can you imagine? It's so completely countercultural that it's *shocking*. The practice of men objectifying women is utterly pervasive these days. Hearing any man describe his wife positively is bound to raise eyebrows. It also provokes an unavoidable question: Why?

Marriage is a sacrament, an outward manifestation of an inner reality that conveys grace. As our primary vocation, it's an indispensable part of our journey to heaven. We take responsibility not just for our journey but also for our wives' journey to get there.

Our wives are priceless gems. We freely chose to make this lifelong commitment to them, and they are worthy of being treasured. They are truly a source of wealth, joy, and contentment.

When we speak of our wives at work, is this the attitude we reflect? Or do we descend into despondent "ball and chain" narratives that are nothing more than prideful self-pity?

Speaking positively about our wives in the workplace has other benefits in addition to the public witness it provides. It also helps *us*. As guys, we're not necessarily known for being "nurturing." However, speaking highly of our wives when they're not around actually helps us nurture the seeds of affection and love in our hearts. It also builds the crucial habit of *thinking* positively about them, leading us to speak positively.

This practice can be difficult if we're going through challenging phases that we all experience from time to time in our marriages. Yet when we're in a challenging phase, it's even *more* critical to honor our wives by not allowing our frustrations to guide our words. Yes, it's acceptable to talk about and address challenges, but only to those who can help, such as a priest, counselor, or spiritual director. When in doubt, talk to your wife and agree upon trusted outsiders who truly have your best interests at heart.

Your wife deserves your respect in the workplace. The two of you—and your coworkers—will benefit from the way you speak about her.

Mindset

Resolve to make your workplace a wife-honoring zone. Decide today that your words, from this time forward, will be positive.

Action Item

Proactively make a positive comment about your spouse to a coworker today.

Speak About Her with Honor at Home

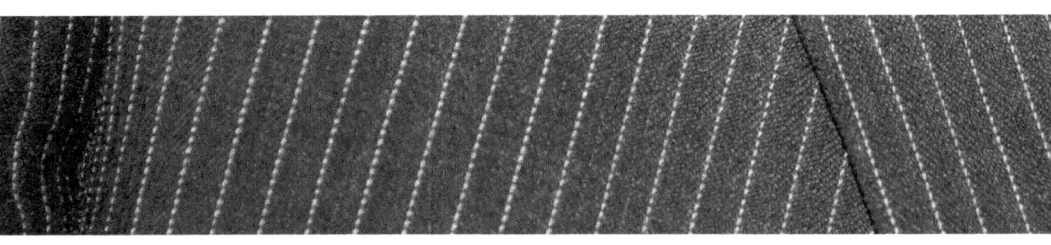

Her children rise up and call her blessed; her husband also, and he praises her:
"Many women have done excellently, but you surpass them all."
— PROVERBS 31:28-29 —

When my second son, T.J., was a teenager, his relationship with Kathi was... at times... umm... *contentious.*

One night, I pulled into the garage and immediately heard a sharp, heated exchange emanating through the door. I reluctantly entered the chaos with a sinking heart. Kathi was crying with vexation. T.J.—red-faced and teeth clenched—was scowling in a corner of the kitchen. Several highly attuned, wide-eyed younger kids were cautiously attempting to play in the family room... at a safe distance.

As it turned out, a stupid, disrespectful comment by T.J. to Kathi had rapidly escalated that night, culminating in the scene I walked into. This wasn't the first conflict of this sort that had erupted between them. I found myself in the uncomfortable position of mediator much more often than I liked.

By the grace of God, I was inspired. "Come with me," I told T.J. We went to a private room and shut the door.

"Dad, she is so unfair!" T.J. exploded, "She doesn't listen to me, and I'm sick of it!"

"We've been over this before," I said. With uncharacteristic patience, I explained that, instead of trying to solve the problem that transpired that night (which differed only in subject matter from the time before that, and the time before that, and so on), we needed a different approach.

"Honor Mom," I told him. "That's your challenge. The circumstances don't matter. If you think she's wrong, it doesn't matter. If you're angry with her, it doesn't matter. You still need to honor Mom."

To this day, T.J. tells me the concept clicked with him during that conversation. It also clicked with me in a different way: it helped me resolve to set the right example, and do my best to speak to my wife with honor in our home. She deserves nothing less.

All families—and by extension all spouses—experience disagreements. However, we have a choice about how we handle those disagreements. In the worst cases, conflicts fester and cause ongoing wounds in our relationships. In the best cases, when we speak to one another with honor and assume positive intent, disagreements catalyze constructive change that strengthens those relationships and builds trust.

I can't overstate the importance of speaking about our wives with honor in the home. It's among the best training we can provide our children. Our sons learn how to treat their wives in the future, and our daughters learn how they should expect to be treated. I'm here to tell you that in the middle of conflict, there's hope that springs from this approach: T.J. calls Kathi now and again these days to thank her for being a terrific mom.

Mindset

Resolve to make your home a wife-honoring zone. Commit to using loving words in the home from this time forward. This means loving words when you feel like it and even when you don't. When necessary, refrain from saying anything when you really want to say something less than loving.

Action Item

Proactively make a positive comment about your spouse to one of your kids today. Yes, even if they're too young to talk. If you don't have kids, another family member will work.

Day 7: Lead Through Sacrifice

And walk in love, as Christ loved us and gave himself up for us,
a fragrant offering and sacrifice to God.
— EPHESIANS 5:2 —

Some guys have a warped sense of leadership within marriage and the family. We sometimes think that as husbands, we're the final authority on everything and that our wives owe us a duty of meek submission. Some think we stop at, "Wives, submit to your husbands." But this is a misleading view of Ephesians 5. Forget about your wife's obligations. Let's focus on ours.

I recently read a book called *The Obedience Paradox: Finding True Freedom in Marriage* by Mary Stanford. It's fantastic! Among other things, the author (who is a speaker, teacher, writer, wife, and mother of seven kids) nails a husband's responsibility in his role within the family:

A husband is called to foster the life—both physical and spiritual—of his wife and children. In preaching to the Ephesians, Saint Paul's use of the head-body image reminds us that any true authority must serve its community, its body, through sacrificial gift. His words did not define a new kind of headship; rather they served to distinguish what characterizes true headship from false and destructive versions. To be head in the manner of Christ himself is, in fact, a return to the concept of authority as life-giving power that we find in the creation account of Genesis. There, all that is comes into being through God's gift. How, then, does Jesus Christ give life to the Church? By pouring out His life for her in a sacrificial offering. (Pages 90-91)

The essence of authentic leadership, then, is what Pope St. John Paul II sometimes referred to as the "gift of self" or "self-gift." We are responsible for the well-being of our wives and children. Again, from Mary Stanford:

He lives his headship most authentically, then, when he possesses a disposition of responsibility and accountability for his family's flourishing. (Page 104)

I love that! And it rings true in my own experience. When Kathi and our children flourish, I feel a deep sense of gratitude and satisfaction. Conversely, when Kathi or one of the kids is struggling or when relationships within the family are strained or fractured, I feel the need to do something about it. When practical solutions are beyond my grasp, which happens more than I'd like, I have a deep sense of responsibility to pray.

Remember, our model in leadership is Jesus, who emptied himself even unto death. Did you ever hear the story of when Jesus demanded that the Church do things his way or else? Of course not, because it never happened. Jesus invites, loves, and gives us his entire self, including his body, blood, soul, and divinity in the Eucharist at Mass. But he never demands that we submit to his authority. Nor should we demand submission. True authority is found in sacrifice.

Mindset

Think about the malformed examples of leadership you've seen in the past, in marriages or families. Consider how situations change with authentic leadership manifested through self-sacrifice. How can you better exemplify Jesus' leadership in your marriage?

Action Item

Do one thing to serve your wife today without being asked. Extra points if it's something you don't like doing. Do it anyway and offer it up for your wife's sanctification.

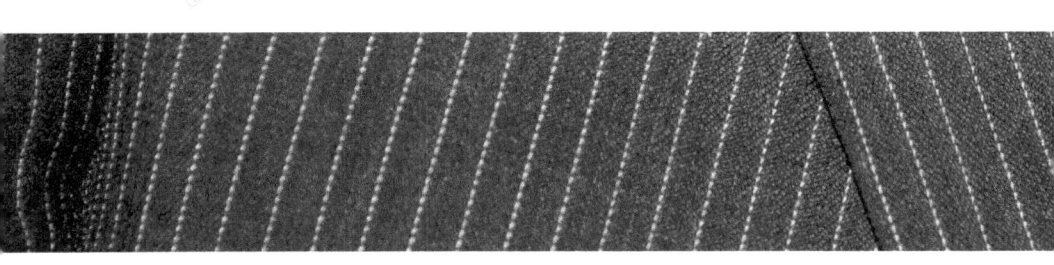

Day 8: Banish Anger

A fool gives full vent to his anger, but a wise man quietly holds it back.
— PROVERBS 29:11 —

Among my greatest regrets is the anger that existed in my family when the oldest kids were little.

We had our first three kids in two years and eight months. No twins, just great chemistry between Kathi and me. I barely remember 1993 due to sleep deprivation. My career in a CPA firm was high-stress, and particularly during tax season the hours required were insane. It seemed like no matter how hard I worked, there was always more to do.

One incident particularly stands out in my mind. Our two boys shared a room next to us in our small, two-bedroom apartment; our infant daughter was in our room. One night, the kids seemed to be taking turns waking up... and waking us up, too. Our oldest son seemed particularly inconsolable. It didn't help that I had a high-pressure business meeting scheduled for the next morning. My career was in its infancy, and as the sole provider for the family, I was desperate to keep it on track.

Sometime around 2 or 3 o'clock in the morning, our oldest son woke up again for about the fifth time. Not even three years old, he screamed with an intensity I couldn't fathom. Exhausted, stressed beyond reason, and utterly spent, I went into his room and gave him a couple swats on his rear end. My wife, herself exhausted, went to console him as even greater misery poured forth, waking up the other babies and making my agony complete.

My wife took our son to the doctor's office the next day. He had an ear infection.

This incident took place decades ago, and it still brings tears to my eyes. I'm heartbroken that in that moment of profound need, my son found an angry, selfish father rather than comfort. I love my son tremendously, and this remains among my worst parenting memories. Regret doesn't even begin to describe how I feel about that night.

Anger, in retrospect, was a desperate attempt to manipulate others within the family. It has also characterized some of the most toxic, unproductive arguments my wife and I have ever had.

Years ago, a new perspective helped us make a shift. Kathi heard a priest talk about anger, and one comment hit her between the eyes: "Anger is a funny emotion. It's there for a reason. God put it there as a reminder of when we need to run to Jesus."

Have you ever hurt those you love as a result of anger? I don't know about you, but through my mistakes, especially early in our marriage,

I have tried hard to become increasingly gentle-hearted toward Kathi and our kids, and now our grandkids. I'm still a work in process, but by grace, I've come a long way. The anger that was common early in our marriage has largely evaporated. It can happen to you, too.

Mindset

Recognize anger as a portal to grave sin and a trap of the devil. It is a destructive force within marriages and families. If this is a weakness for you, it's an extremely worthy and profitable struggle to engage.

Action Item

Take your intention to banish anger to prayer. Go to confession. Seek the Blessed Sacrament in adoration. Listen and firmly resolve to change. If you need further help, consider counseling to make behavioral changes that will benefit you and radiate outwards.

Day 9: Where Are Your Eyes?

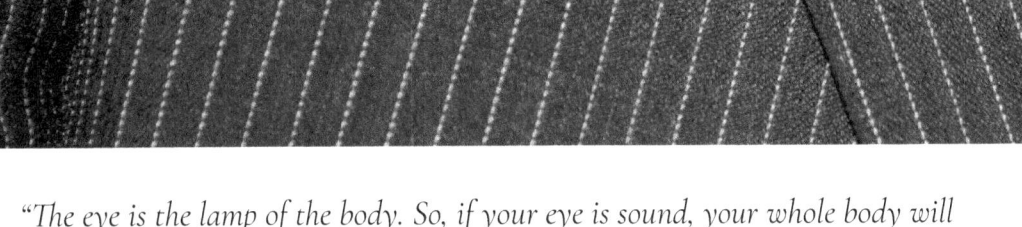

"The eye is the lamp of the body. So, if your eye is sound, your whole body will be full of light; but if your eye is not sound, your whole body will be full of darkness. If then the light in you is darkness, how great is the darkness!"
— MATTHEW 6:22-23 —

I've attended "evenings of recollection" over the years given by a wonderful priest, Fr. Joe. He's famous for his witty one-liners, and a few have stuck with me. Among his favorite topics when speaking to an audience of men is what he calls "custody of the eyes." He'll give the example of a pretty young woman jogging down the street toward us. "Where are your eyes?" he roars. Lowered heads acknowledge the problem.

Men tend to be visual creatures. Is that true for you? If so, did it spontaneously change when you got married?

Didn't think so.

In the Sermon on the Mount, Jesus speaks explicitly about the downfalls of letting this temptation get the best of us. Matthew 5:27-28 says, "You have heard that it was said, 'You shall not commit adultery.' But I say to you that every one who looks at a woman lustfully has already committed adultery with her in his heart."

Compare this to what might be called the conventional "wisdom" of our secular culture. Have you ever heard a guy say, "I can look at the menu anywhere, so long as I eat at home"? In other words, it's okay to lust after other women so long as you don't cheat on your wife. Wrong! According to Jesus, you have committed adultery, a grave sin.

So what's a guy to do? If we want to honor our wives, we must develop a discipline that begins in our minds. We will invariably see attractive women in our daily lives. Seeing them is not an issue. The problem is when we indulge in looking at them with lust in our hearts. I know a priest (who is still a man, after all) who says in his mind, *Hello, pretty lady*, since he recognizes that the source of this woman's beauty is God. He then averts his gaze.

Another technique is redirection. For a married guy, that means seeing an attractive woman and taking that as a signal to think of his wife instead. Of course, you should avoid developing a spirit of lust toward your wife, but it's healthy to be sexually attracted to her. As your wife, she is the only one worthy of that attraction.

One of the best ways to safeguard our hearts is to safeguard our minds. If we're focused too much on the wrong thing (or the wrong person), we have an absolute responsibility to change and truly honor our wives.

Mindset

Commit to the scriptural teaching that custody of your eyes is essential in helping you better honor your wife. Focus on her, not others.

Action Item

Next time you see your wife, take a good look at her. Then, pick one of her most attractive qualities and tell her what it is.

Day 10: Protect Your Marriage

"So they are no longer two but one.
What therefore God has joined together, let not man put asunder."
— MATTHEW 19:6 —

"Want to grab lunch?"

Momentarily disoriented, I looked up from my desk to see the smiling face of my coworker, Jane. It was an innocent request, but my face flushed, and I nervously looked at my computer, checking my calendar while my mind raced furiously.

After an embarrassingly long pause, I managed to stammer, "You-you know, I'm really kinda busy today. I was going to grab something quick, want me to bring something back?"

That wasn't entirely truthful. It was, however, the best I could manage on short notice.

Why didn't I go to lunch with Jane? It had nothing to do with her; it was all about Kathi. Early in our marriage, Kathi and I went through periods of disillusionment and found ourselves unwittingly in vulnerable positions. Critical of one another's faults, it was all too easy to imagine ourselves with someone else. We both drifted into places where we began to admire—and were attracted to—other people. Idealized people. They didn't have the familiar, grating negatives we saw in one another.

By the grace of God, we caught ourselves early in the process, confessed the problem to one another, and recommitted ourselves to our marriage. Sadly, we knew friends who failed to prevent this problem, which began with friendship and proceeded to disordered emotional intimacy. If not stopped in time, this idealization causes a slippery slope toward an affair and even the disintegration of a marriage and family.

That is why I decided not to go to lunch alone with women who are not my wife. I'm all for group lunches, and professional friendships in the workplace with members of the opposite sex are often healthy and normal. Yet I have learned that one way I can honor my wife is to build a protective wall around our marriage; in other words, emotional and physical intimacy is for her alone. This approach has increased the trust between the two of us.

If you have questions about how this should play out in practice, ask yourself, "How would I act if my wife was sitting right next to me?" Would you complain about your wife to a female coworker if your wife was in the chair next to you? I bet not! I'll also bet that your words about your wife would honor her, as discussed previously.

Remember your eyes, another previous topic. One of the most memorable incidents in my career was when a female coworker was leaving the firm we both worked for, and she thanked me for routinely looking at her eyes rather than her chest. Apparently, that wasn't always the case with a couple of guys in the office. I was stunned.

I did loop back around with Jane, by the way. She understood completely.

Mindset

Marriage is exclusive, and that exclusivity makes it worth protecting. Even when things aren't going well, we need to recommit ourselves (daily) to protecting it.

Action Item

Write down one area where you could improve the protection of your marriage. Keep it on your daily to-do list for at least the next month.

Day 11: Practice Gratitude

This is the day which the LORD has made; let us rejoice and be glad in it.
— PSALM 118:24 —

From time to time, adjustments are needed in the way we communicate with others. I recall a phase (when all eight of our kids lived at home) when there was a lot of bickering among family members... *all of us.* Verbal jabs, sarcastic comments, and accusations had somehow become routine forms of communication.

"But wait," I thought. "We're a family. We love one another. We can do better than this."

The solution? Every night after dinner, we began to go around the table. Each of us would identify at least one thing we were grateful for about another family member. It could be something they had done or a character quality we appreciated.

"I'm grateful to Mom for making my favorite dinner tonight."

47

"I'm grateful to Christian for being patient with me and helping me with my homework today."

"I'm grateful for T.J.'s terrific sense of humor."

And on it went.

Although it felt awkward initially, we all improved quickly. The younger kids, especially, proved to be gratitude rock stars. Over time this exercise helped the culture of our family to become more positive, humble, and supportive.

We can do the same thing with our wives. By cultivating an attitude of gratitude, we can gradually get better at ensuring that our wives are held in the proper esteem. After all, aren't they the greatest gift God has given us, second only to our faith?

I've watched friends and family members who have lost their wives struggle to their core to cope with the loss. It's as if they've had part of their bodies amputated, and their grief is palpable. In the throes of this excruciating experience, I recall an uncle of mine encouraging me to treasure the time I have with my wife, admonishing me to "tell her you love her constantly."

Have you ever noticed that focusing on what we lack breeds misery? Conversely, appreciating what we do have makes us happy. This discipline of striving for gratitude toward our wives helps our well-being. Personally, I consider my wife an incredible treasure and gift.

Mindset

A gratitude mindset involves focusing on the good qualities in your wife *right now*. They exist, even in moments of pain or struggle. Gratitude is essential to keep our minds balanced and recognize her for the enduring gift she is.

Action Item

Set an alarm once a day, and when it goes off, think of just one reason you're grateful for your wife. Then tell her.

Day 12:

Prioritize Her Above Work

Let the favor of the Lord our God be upon us, and establish the work of our hands upon us, yes, establish the work of our hands.
— PSALM 90:17 —

My wife got run off the road a while back.

Some guy was in a big hurry and didn't like that Kathi had slowed down to merge onto the highway behind a school bus full of children. He accelerated from behind and drove up beside her, forcing her onto the berm. After almost causing multiple accidents, he suddenly veered to the right and exited precisely five cars in front of her further down the highway. Unbelievable.

He was so focused on achieving his objective (whatever it was) that he risked carnage and mayhem. If things went badly, innocent people could have been hurt.

In thinking about this incident, I was struck by the thought that the same could be true if men develop a disordered dedication to work.

That sounds nutty, right? But how many of us struggle with work-family balance? And how many people do you know who are divorced because of ridiculous work schedules?

Kathi and I struggled mightily in this area. When we were young parents, I worked ludicrous hours. My schedule at the CPA firm was grueling, and our first three kids came along very quickly. On top of it all, Kathi had premature labor with our third child and was on strict bedrest for the last four months of the pregnancy.

After our daughter was born, it became apparent that the work-family balance thing wasn't working, especially as I headed into tax season. I'm crazy about my wife, but it probably didn't feel like it to her at the time. I wasn't spending enough time at home to meet my responsibilities as her husband. That was the first time we hit a wall. I don't recall her exact words, but Kathi said something like, "It's either the job or me."

I chose her and changed jobs.

I'm glad I chose her, and through her, I also chose our kids.

Fast forward a few years, and I was working like a maniac again. Kathi was expecting our seventh child, but there were medical problems. We weren't sure the baby would make it past birth this time. Beyond that, the diagnosis was uncertain at best. It seemed like life was spinning out of control. It was another decision point.

Again, I chose her (and the baby) and changed jobs.

Don't get me wrong. The changes we made took time. The process was messy, and we struggled with uncertainty, conflict, and self-doubt.

We prayed fervently, discussed possible solutions, and consulted with trusted priests, family members, and friends. Changing jobs isn't always the right answer, but it's what we needed. More to the point, it's what *she* needed: she yearned for stability and greater predictability in my schedule.

Predictability = Stability. It's not always possible, but that's what Kathi needed from me at that point in our lives. By prioritizing her needs over my own ambitions at work, I gave her what she needed.

In doing so, this took me off the path to becoming a partner at my CPA firm, a dream I had held onto for years. Ultimately, the career change led me down a more rewarding career path that wouldn't have happened otherwise. By the grace of God, it all worked out: my career, my marriage, and kid number seven, who is now in his 20s and doing great. While some of the medical issues are ongoing, he is a blessing beyond measure to our entire family.

Mindset

We often experience challenging times in our careers, and it's not always possible to provide predictability or work fewer hours. However, if work is consistently prioritized above our wives' and families' needs, it's a matter for prayer and reflection.

Action Item

Set aside regular one-on-one time for your wife and ask her what attention she needs (such as listening without problem-solving, emotional support, affection, etc.) so she feels truly prioritized.

Day 13: Give Her Children

But Jesus said, "Let the children come to me, and do not hinder them;
for to such belongs the kingdom of heaven."
— MATTHEW 19:14 —

I couldn't help but overhear the conversation just outside my office. "Yeah, I'm not sure whether I want another baby. One day, I think yes; the next day, not so much." Andrea was speaking with a couple of other colleagues standing nearby, who nodded sympathetically.

Exiting my office, I smiled at the group, and they immediately burst out laughing. They probably figured that I had an opinion on the subject. In a secular workplace, I was something of a curiosity. After all, why would anyone want eight kids?

Of course, each couple decides how many kids to have. I don't impart any unsolicited advice on the subject, even with my adult children. We encourage them to discern this together prayerfully. That said, I have a few thoughts I'm willing to share.

First, the ability to have children is a tremendous gift. Many people have not received this gift, which can often be a source of sadness and disappointment. Throughout scripture, children are regarded as a blessing, and I couldn't agree more. Even when kids do stupid things (a singular element of accomplishment in my youth), they have inestimable, eternal value.

People often regret not having kids or not having more kids once they're past childbearing age. My young colleagues were in the most difficult years, with young children at home. Those years don't last forever; it does get easier. Frankly, I look back with amazement that Kathi and I were able to manage eight kids somehow. Yet now that they're all older, many with children of their own, I can't imagine a greater blessing.

When I was young, we used to have a huge birthday bash for my paternal grandmother every five years. She was the mother of six children, my dad being the youngest. At her 85th birthday party, I remember being struck by how many people existed because of this one woman. Six children had numerous children of their own, who had begun, in turn, to have families. Surveying the hundred or so people in a big hotel ballroom that night, around half of them were direct descendants of my grandmother. God bless her.

I now see the same phenomenon emanating from my beloved wife. Her desire for children was good. While I occasionally felt overwhelmed by the responsibility to provide for our growing brood, it was worth it.

It was all worth it.

Yes, with fewer kids, my retirement account might be larger. But our greatest source of wealth is our family: our marriage, our children, our grandchildren, and on and on it will go. The *Catechism of the Catholic Church* reminds us clearly about the purpose of marriage:

> By its very nature it is ordered to the good of the couple, as well as to the generation and education of children. (CCC 1660)

If your wife wants children, consider it prayerfully and responsibly. Yes, it will be a challenge. Be not afraid. It's worth it.

Mindset

Parenthood helps bring us out of ourselves and become other-centered in a commendable way. We won't be perfect, but it's a worthy challenge that we can meet with God's grace.

Action Item

Talk to your wife about her dreams, desires, fears, and hopes about children. How can you support her and together discern God's will for your family?

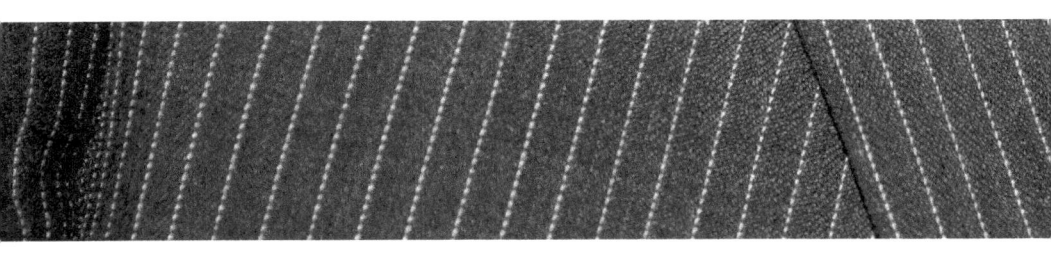

Day 14: Respect Her Freedom

For freedom Christ has set us free;
stand fast therefore, and do not submit again to a yoke of slavery.
— GALATIANS 5:1 —

Marriage is not a form of slavery. It's a sad commentary that some people seem to think of it that way and go to great lengths to avoid the commitment that comes with it. Properly understood, marriage leads to greater freedom, not bondage.

Dr. Scott Hahn, a noted theologian and friend, has done compelling work on the nature of covenant, and how it entails an exchange of persons, making it distinct from a legal contract. In other words, when we get married, we exchange persons by giving ourselves wholly and completely to our spouse. According to scripture, we become "one flesh." This is a spiritual reality and a practical reality.

How does this work? I'll leave the spiritual side to the theologians, but the practical side is all about complementarity. As I mentioned in a previous chapter, the husband and wife can play off one another's strengths for mutual benefit. Essentially, we're a team where the sum of the whole is greater than its parts. How does this impact the freedom of spouses? To be clear, freedom is not a license to do whatever we want. Here's what the *Catechism of the Catholic Church* has to say:

> *Freedom is the power, rooted in reason and will, to act or not to act, to do this or that, and so to perform deliberate actions on one's own responsibility. By free will one shapes one's own life. Human freedom is a force for growth and maturity in truth and goodness; it attains its perfection when directed toward God, our beatitude. (CCC, 1731)*

There's no exception for marriage here. At our best, we act in a way that directs our efforts toward God. Alas, we're not always at our best. Temptations abound when it comes to directing our efforts—and attempting to help direct our spouse's efforts—toward ourselves rather than God. Have you ever fallen into this trap? I sure have.

Kathi's grandmother lived to be 102 years old, and just recently passed. She was among the most remarkable people I have known, and she constantly amazed us with her resilience, wisdom, and love for our family. We always tried to visit as often as possible, but those desires were sometimes frustrated by the two-and-a-half-hour drive.

One weekend, Kathi wanted to visit Grandma. Usually, I would have fully supported her, but I was physically and emotionally spent that weekend and looking forward to slowing down. I wanted to spend time with Kathi and perhaps take her on a date. I eventually relented, but it took a while.

There is a spectrum of possible responses to such a situation, and I've been guilty of some of the less charitable ones in our more distant past. It's something I've also witnessed in other marriages over the years, and on some occasions, I've seen even worse responses than my own: attempts to use guilt, emotional pressure, withholding love and affection, or other manipulative tactics to get one's way.

You've heard of controlling spouses, right? That's what we're trying to avoid.

Thankfully, I had a great example in my father, and over the years I watched him studiously respect my mom's freedom. It's not like my parents agreed on everything, but they always talked through situations that arose; if my dad could support my mom, he did. In one instance out of thousands, I recall my dad springing for a used potter's wheel and kiln for my mom so she could have a hobby. This involved real sacrifice since money wasn't plentiful, but my dad derived great satisfaction in his ability to support my mom. I now experience that same fulfillment by supporting Kathi.

In many ways, manipulation for our selfish ends and controlling behavior are antithetical to true love that always desires the good of the other. That's why freedom in marriage is so important. We're here to support one another, not to make decisions on behalf of the other for our own benefit. If this is a trap you've ever fallen into, know that there's hope. By respecting our wife's freedom, we can recognize what the *Catechism* beautifully describes as *"a force for growth and maturity in truth and goodness."* (CCC 1731)

Mindset

Freedom involves a deep respect for our spouses and a desire for their good. That precludes the need to pressure or manipulate them.

Action Item

Talk through the next contentious issue that arises in your marriage and consciously respect your wife's freedom throughout the discussion.

Day 15: Renew Your Commitment

On the third day there was a marriage at Cana in Galilee, and the mother of Jesus was there; Jesus also was invited to the marriage, with his disciples.

— JOHN 2:1-2 —

Do you remember your marriage vows? If you were married in the Church, there are a couple of variations, but they probably went something like this:

> *I take you for my lawful wife, to have and to hold from this day forward, for better, for worse, for richer, for poorer, in sickness and in health, until death do us part.*

For those who have been married for a while, attending weddings is a great reminder that these vows really mean something. I've always appreciated the "for better, for worse, for richer, for poorer, in sickness and in health" parts since Kathi and I have experienced all those situations in our journey.

If you've been married for any length of time, one way to mark special anniversaries is to recommit to your vows. Kathi and I did this a few years ago to celebrate our 30th anniversary, and it was powerful. Our parish priest performed the rites after Mass. There's something profound and deeply moving about the ceremony: the words, the blessings, and the reminder of the sacramental and practical significance of marriage.

It's worth periodically reflecting on your marriage vows and the importance of persevering through life's inevitable ups and downs. Honoring these vows honors our spouses.

Marriages are such tremendous sources of grace, and the Lord has frequently spoken—and continues to speak—through my wife. She knows me better than any other human being on this planet, and our marriage covenant has been instrumental in helping me to advance along the path of humility, holiness, and charity. Has your marriage helped you to become a better Christian? That's what God intended.

Marriage is also a vocation, a holy calling that helps us along the path of sanctification and growth in charity. Why is this important? Partly because it provides the foundational context for our earthly lives, which are invariably finite. I've never heard it as a point of great emphasis, but the "until death do us part" line in the vows suggests a finish line for the marriage, even if not for our immortal souls.

To put it bluntly, we're all going to die at some point. At that moment, our marriages are over. Not in a bad way, mind you, but in the sense that this vocation... this bond... this way of living has been brought to its natural fulfillment. A successful fulfillment, so help us God! But what is a successful fulfillment, precisely? For both spouses to become saints! And in the divine plan, our marriages are designed to help us get there.

Our vows matter, and recommitting to them helps reinvigorate our commitment to our spouses.

Mindset

Recommit yourself to your marriage vows by revisiting them periodically and recommitting to them privately and prayerfully even more frequently. Honoring your vows honors your wife.

Action Item

Get creative and consider a fun way to ask about making "the ask" about a recommitment to your vows. Think of it as a mini-marriage proposal.

Be Present to Her

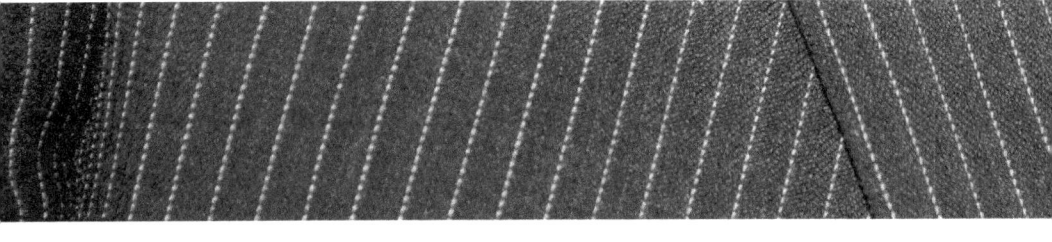

Husbands, love your wives, and do not be harsh with them.
— COLOSSIANS 3:19 —

"Why don't you put your jacket in the suitcase? You won't need it once we get to Miami." Having finally arrived at the airline check-in, Kathi's suggestion was a bit of a forehead smacker. *Well, yeah,* I thought. *Of course!* We were headed out on a long-awaited vacation and looked forward to decidedly un-Central Ohio-like December weather.

"Make sure to check your pockets." Again, the practical side of my brain (Kathi) spoke up. Once again, eminently reasonable. I checked—left pocket, then right pocket—before hurriedly stuffing my jacket into the suitcase. I smiled at the friendly airline agent while heaving the heavy suitcase onto the baggage scale.

Except that my jacket has three pockets.

As we were winding our way toward the security checkpoint, I froze. Where's my cell phone? In a millisecond, the sequence of events flashed before my eyes. Panicked, I realized that my cell phone—with way too much of the contents of my life therein—was headed merrily to Miami in the breast pocket of my jacket. In my suitcase. That I had just checked.

It took a minute to recover from the shock, but after a brief conferral with Kathi, we agreed it wasn't a complete disaster. The friendly airline agent provided old-school paper boarding passes, so we were good there. I had forgotten to bring the book about St. Frances Cabrini that I had brought along for the trip, which was more of a conventional oversight, but that could wait. But what was I going to do for the next several hours? No email, music, texting, phone calls, or news. No pictures. No airline apps. No... Internet?!

By the grace of God, I offered up my little self-imposed exile from electronic connectedness and decided to make the most of it. What followed convicted me. Did you know there's a whole world out there that's not on your phone? Apparently, *I* had forgotten!

Over the next several hours, I was (somewhat uncomfortably at first) forced to be present. One of the first things I noticed was that everyone around me was absorbed in their cell phones!

I decided to seize the opportunity and pray for people. I prayed for the frazzled dad trying to wrangle his young son during a meltdown; the sad woman across the aisle who appeared to have the weight of the world on her shoulders; the stressed-out couple speaking in low but sharp tones to one another; and the young mom in front of me trying to keep her daughter quiet as the youngster expressed her frustration with indistinct shrieks and glares of indignation toward her mother.

The latter pair caught my attention. With great affection, the mother gently and lovingly redirected and encouraged her daughter, who had developmental challenges. She showered her daughter with attention and astonishing levels of patience. It reminded me of my wife, who had so often demonstrated these qualities with our children.

As we exited the airplane, I caught up with the mom. "You have a beautiful daughter, and she's lucky to have you as her mom," I told her.

"Thank you, I appreciate you saying that," was the slightly startled response. Her smile was all the thanks I needed.

It was like traveling back a couple of decades, and what I wish my wife could have heard–maybe from a stranger, but certainly she should have heard it from me. I regret that I didn't do a better job expressing my appreciation for my wife's heroic efforts on behalf of our kids. But then again, I wasn't always present. Whether it was work, self-absorption, or my phone (or did I mention work?), I should have done a better job of being present. I still struggle with it. If I hadn't sent my phone on a detour that day, *I might not have even noticed.*

Mindset

Are we present to our wives and the other loved ones in our lives? Jesus, as always, is our model. He was present to each person he encountered. Our wives are more important than anything on our phones!

Action Item

Resolve to set aside your phone regularly when you spend time with your wife. She deserves your full attention and presence. I'll do my best too!

Help Her Breathe

*Jesus said to him, "I am the way, and the truth, and the life;
no one comes to the Father, but by me.*
— JOHN 14:6 —

Have I mentioned that my wife is incredible? It never ceases to amaze me how precisely her gifts align with my needs. (I sure hope that goes both ways!) My financial background, for example, is very helpful in certain ways. Yet Kathi's nursing education has been invaluable. It might have even saved my life.

Kathi and I were out on a dinner date at our local Mexican restaurant. I love Mexican food, and we both have our favorite dishes. As with many long-time couples, we know what the other enjoys and end up sharing parts of our meals accordingly. This evening, Kathi generously offered me some of her refried beans. (Pro tip: they're awesome with nacho chips).

I obligingly grabbed the nearest chip and loaded it up with a generous helping of beans while wolfing down my favorite steak burrito. I swallowed, and the food didn't go down. Panicked, I swallowed again.

No movement. With a steak burrito lodged in my throat and a heavy chip quickly thrown down onto the table, I glanced at her, wide-eyed, while trying unsuccessfully to inhale.

"Are you choking?" she asked gently. I nodded. "It's okay, just relax. Let me know if you need my help."

At that moment, prompted by her soft voice, I realized she was exactly right. I immediately did my best to straighten my neck and relax my throat to provide a better pathway for air. Although it took a few moments—that felt like an *hour*—I filled my lungs with air and swallowed the food successfully before taking a sip of water. Eyes watering, embarrassed, and hoping I hadn't created a scene, Kathi's tender coaching got me through what felt pretty traumatic at the time. As I write this, I'm involuntarily inhaling deeply, perhaps subconsciously rejoicing in my ability to breathe freely.

Reflecting on this event, I'm grateful for Kathi's presence beside me at the restaurant. Later, she told me that she knew what to do if I had continued choking, and I believed her. Yet it struck me that I have a parallel responsibility for her. I need to help her breathe, too.

What does that mean? I can only hope I would reciprocate Kathi's calm demeanor if she choked at a restaurant, but there's a deeper calling within marriage that goes beyond the practical.

The "air" that our wives need to sustain life, both now and into eternity, is Jesus Christ himself and the sacramental life of the Church he founded. Jesus is our model for being a good husband; he is our perfect example of love. As the scripture verse at the beginning of the chapter states, he is "the way and the truth and the life." Part of our most solemn responsibility on this earth—and one central to our vocation as husbands—is to act as Christ to our wives and follow his example to the best of our poor abilities.

Not confident you're up to that? Thankfully, you're not alone. And you're not without tools to get the job done.

That's where the Church comes in. Jesus didn't just come to earth for a few years, die, rise again, and leave us to our own devices. We join in his divine life with the Father and the Holy Spirit through the sacraments. This is the "air" our wives need. In my humble opinion, the Church provides an incomparable context for human flourishing, since the God of the universe created the Church and the sacraments just for us.

When we or our wives feel like we're choking—literally or figuratively— we need to remember that our natural response to panic won't help. We need to breathe and to trust. Trust Jesus, who loves us and our wives more than we can imagine. Trust the Church's sacraments to be fruitful even through life's most difficult trials. Embrace Christ and his Church for your life, your wife's life, and your marriage. Breathe!

Mindset

Recognize the Catholic faith as the oxygen you and your wife need to flourish. The Church is full of imperfect people like us, but it also gives us sustenance for life from Jesus himself.

Action Item

Lead your wife spiritually by setting the right example. Consistently take her to Mass, model frequent confession, pray with her, gift her a retreat, and treasure and protect her spiritual life.

Be Humble

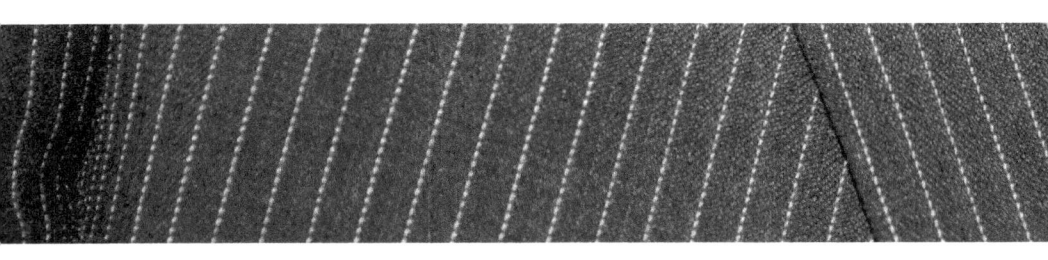

When pride comes, then comes disgrace; but with the humble is wisdom.
— PROVERBS 11:2 —

Has your attention ever been inexplicably drawn to someone? Or have thoughts about someone randomly pop up? A stranger or a friend, perhaps someone you see walking down the street, remember from the past, or even think about in the middle of the night when you can't sleep? As Christians, we're given the tools to help others along life's journey, and that starts with our prayers. When someone is on our minds, we are invited to pray for them.

One prayer I like to say is, "Lord Jesus, please help that person and me to become good friends in heaven." Now, I get that it's a prayer for me just as much as them. But if we believe in the power of prayer, we should do it constantly, as St. Paul instructs us in 1 Thessalonians 5. If this is true for others, shouldn't it be even more important for your wife? Her eternal friendship is part of your life's work and our mission as husbands.

Yet, focusing too much on ourselves hinders that mission. What's the antidote? Humility. Although not a fashionable virtue these days, growing in humility can provide a strategic advantage for your marriage to reach new heights.

C.S. Lewis said humility isn't thinking less of ourselves, but thinking of ourselves less. I decided to put this into practice when Kathi and I went on a vacation together a few years ago. Unlike previous vacations, where I had been more focused on relaxing and having a good time, I decided to go out of my way to help *her* relax and have a good time. It became one of the best vacations we've ever had... and even *more* enjoyable for me! Of course, you don't need to wait for vacation to put this into practice; it can be done daily. By focusing on your wife's needs, you both benefit.

There are other benefits, too. One of the best ways to build your marriage is to increase trust. Trust grows through our willingness to be vulnerable, which requires humility.

I've often thought of marriage as the underrated sacrament. When we talk about frequenting the sacraments, we usually speak of receiving the Eucharist or the Sacrament of Reconciliation. But marriage is also a sacrament, and one that is central to our calling and lived out twenty-four/seven. My wife sometimes tells me jokingly that the Holy Spirit speaks through wives. While she's kidding, she isn't wrong.

To appreciate Kathi, treasure our marriage, and listen to her as if the Holy Spirit is speaking through her, I need to be humble and truly focus on her. That means I need to listen to what she's trying to express through her words and actions; ask for clarification if needed; resolve to reflect upon what she's saying; not be dismissive; and appreciate the different perspective she brings. In short, I need to grow in humility.

I get that growing in humility is a steep hill to climb. It doesn't come naturally to any of us. When was the last time you met a humble three-year-old? We spend our lives looking through our own eyes, and you probably never took Humility 101 in college, either. Thankfully, there are some good examples of humble people. Too often we see the opposite. Particularly toxic is the wasteland of anonymous comments on the internet, spewing hubris and treating other human beings in appalling ways.

While we can't fix the internet or other people's hearts, we can pray and resolve to take steps toward our own humility. It's an incredibly attractive virtue that our culture—and our wives—yearn for.

Mindset

Resolve to grow in humility and pray for the grace to do so.

Action Item

Take an hour and do something that you know your wife would appreciate: Wash her car. Clean out the refrigerator. Write her a note of appreciation. Buy her flowers.

Be Her Friend

A faithful friend is an elixir of life; and those who fear the Lord will find him.
— Sirach 6:16 —

I am blessed to have a dear friend named Gary, whom I've known for over 20 years. We've worked together at two companies and shared countless highs and lows in our professional and personal lives. Happily, we've also shared countless meals along the way, particularly at our favorite Mexican restaurant.

We "married up" because we both have awesome and better wives than we deserve. In addition to being foreign-born (Gary's from Ireland, and I'm from Canada), we're both tall, and we both live in the U.S. because of our aforementioned wives. We kid around that our stories both started with "Well, there was this girl..."

We both have a gaggle of kids, an enthusiasm for cars, and a love for our Church. At our most recent company, we often paused to pray a Divine Mercy Chaplet for our families and those we worked with.

Gary is a faithful friend, and I thoroughly enjoy his company. It's a privilege to count him as a friend. He's also among a slowly dwindling number of good friends I've literally known for decades. As the song goes, you can't make old friends. We have a finite number of good friends in this life, and I have hope that those special friendships continue in eternity.

The scripture verse from Sirach at the beginning of this chapter calls faithful friends the "elixir of life." What does an elixir do for us? It prolongs life and acts as a cure-all. According to Greek philosophy, there are four types of love, and the one particular to friendship is called *philia*.

Philia is characterized by affection, respect, high regard, support, and being on good terms.

I know this doesn't describe every second of every day with our wives, but it's something to shoot for. Among the essential building blocks of a strong marriage is the element of friendship. We need to be our wife's best friend. As much as I enjoy spending time with Gary, there's always one person I enjoy spending time with even more: Kathi. I think that's the way it's supposed to be.

Kathi and I were married young: I was 22, and she was barely 20. We've experienced a lot of *life* together, including individual and shared triumphs and sorrows. We have had children born, relatives and friends pass away, weddings, graduations, birthdays, excitement, and boredom.

Now in our 50's, our friendship has deepened immeasurably over time. We enjoy sitting together in front of the fireplace, drinking coffee, and talking. We walk—sometimes miles at a time—and that's often when we have our most meaningful conversations. We go out for meals together or make something at home. It doesn't need to be fancy. In fact, during the writing of this chapter, I took a quick break to make her some cinnamon-raisin toast with a bit of whipped cream cheese, along with the required Coke Zero... in the proper container, with crushed ice and a straw, because I know that's how she likes it.

(I highly recommend the cinnamon-raisin toast with cream cheese, by the way. It'll change your life.)

Of course, there are impediments to nurturing a good friendship with our wives. In my case, the biggest threat has always been professional busyness, but that's only the top hit of a long list. Other factors people may encounter include the stresses of life, unresolved conflict, lack of trust, fear of rejection, a critical spirit, and a lack of intentionality. Yet all these can be overcome with a concrete commitment to be your wife's best friend, prioritize her, and spend the time together that you both need for your friendship and marriage to flourish.

Mindset

Even if it feels a little strange at first, set aside time with your wife to be her friend.

Action Item

Make her a snack of her favorite thing, prepared just the way she likes it. Or re-connect by intentionally taking the time to do an activity that you both enjoy as best friends.

Listen

A fool takes no pleasure in understanding, but only in expressing his opinion.
— PROVERBS 18:2 —

I don't know about you, but I believe listening is one of the most important marital skills for husbands. Not many of us are good at it, and I am at the front of the line for remedial help. Over the last 35 years, my lack of listening skills has probably started more arguments with Kathi than any of the items on my long list of faults.

One of our first arguments is still memorable to me. Within the first couple of months, during our otherwise blissful newlywed stage, we exchanged heated words over a singularly unimportant topic: how to fold towels.

(Come to think of it, I still think of us as being in the newlywed stage. Wonder when that ends? But I digress...)

I folded towels the way my mother had instructed me as a reluctant teenager. My method wasn't pretty, but it was fast. Why take too much time folding towels, with so many other and more important things to do?

Kathi wasn't having it. "No, do it this way!" came the sharp rebuke. "This way, it fits on the towel rack better."

I wasn't buying that line of thinking. "Your way takes forever!" I protested. "This isn't an art project; we're just going to use them and throw them back in the hamper anyway."

Kathi's glowering responses seemed to indicate a curiously high level of emotion as the discussion devolved into a pained silence. "I'll just do it myself," she said. With that, she picked up the hamper and went into the next room.

I was left slightly bewildered. What had I done wrong? I was only trying to help with the stupid laundry. I had inadvertently jabbed an emotional hot button that wasn't labeled and didn't have a name. The inner forces of self-pity were strong in my logical-brain narrative.

This is not uncommon among newly married couples. Integrating two people and two distinct family cultures takes time, patience, and mutual understanding, but I wasn't exactly an exemplar of those attributes on that particular day.

Among my faults was not listening. Not really, anyway. I heard the words, certainly, but got ouchy instead of making the effort to understand what Kathi was trying to explain. In later (and unfortunately tearful) conversations, I started to grasp the larger issues in play. She had single-handedly taken the responsibility of doing the laundry. My level of responsibility-taking at that point wasn't quite comparable, and she felt devalued and disrespected. Almost without realizing it, my counterpoint had been overly critical of her and hadn't stayed on the topic of laundry but strayed more broadly into other areas.

Keeping on point is such an important element of resolving conflict. Because of this influential argument, which happened when we lived in Cleveland, we now remind one another to "stay in Cleveland" when one of us strays from the topic. This helps to keep the argument on point and prevent unnecessary escalation.

My other tendency—and I'm pretty sure this is true of a lot of guys—is that I tend to over-solve problems. Sometimes, my wife needs me to shut up and listen. That means taking the time to understand and ask clarifying questions, and don't offer brilliant solutions unless they're requested. That's hard for me, and I'm still working on it.

Listening is an important life skill, and a gift to your wife. It's worth working on our listening skills; they will pay dividends for the rest of our lives.

Mindset

If you're unsure whether your wife wants you to solve a problem or listen, ask her.

Action Item

Resolve to have one entire conversation with your wife without offering a single possible solution. Take your brain out of "fix it" gear, put it into "empathetic overdrive," and ask questions. Just listen and love her.

Day 21: Ask For Forgiveness

Therefore confess your sins to one another, and pray for one another, that you may be healed. The prayer of a righteous man has great power in its effects.
— JAMES 5:16 —

I'm originally from the Toronto, Canada area. When I was a kid, my dad was a minister, and I was a "P.K." or "Preacher's Kid."* Consistent with the P.K. stereotype, I was rebellious during my teen years. My behavior was lamentable and occasionally dreadful. Frequently regrettable. Intermittently appalling. I was bad.

As a result, I found myself in a boarding school for the last two years of high school. Thankfully, it turned into an excellent experience. I enjoyed the rigorous hockey program, tolerated the outstanding academic training (which, despite my protests, was a huge benefit,) and befriended classmates from across the globe.

---

* Yes, I'm Catholic now (and so is my dad). For details on that cosmic transformation, see my book *How God Hauled Me Kicking and Screaming into the Catholic Church* (Our Sunday Visitor, 2016).

One of my best friends was from Nigeria. I'll never forget one of the first days he had to walk in the snow and quickly landed on his backside. I joked about needing to teach him how to walk like a Canadian. He was not amused, but there is a technique to it. Besides proper footwear (that my friend didn't have), when you walk on slippery snow or ice, it's important to walk a bit flat-footed to keep your balance. Try it, you'll see.

Aside from walking carefully on snow, another distinctive thing about Canadians is, well, I'm sorry, but we apologize constantly. That's not all bad, though, because it helped prepare me for marriage.

Over the last 35 years I have apologized a lot more than I expected. Do you ever tell your wife you're sorry for something you've done or said? I have. Countless times. None of us is perfect, and most probably need to apologize more rather than less.

Having said that, there are some things we need to consider when it comes to apologies. I don't know many husbands who over-apologize, but there is always a danger that we might cheapen our apologies if they're reflexive rather than substantive.

If we seldom apologize, there's something wrong with that, too. I don't know many husbands who never have reason to say that they're sorry to their wives.

One way to become better at apologizing is to look no further than the Sacrament of Confession. What better model could there be for apologizing to our wives than apologizing to God?

The first step is an examination of conscience. What is on your conscience that you should apologize about? In some cases, you'll know immediately. Maybe she'll even tell you immediately! In other cases, perhaps some interaction is on your mind that you feel badly about.

Next, it's essential that you are sorry. Your wife intuitively knows whether this is the case. If you're saying "sorry" to escape negative consequences, that won't cut it. That's why a sacramental confession requires what's called a "firm purpose of amendment" or resolve to change your behavior. So when apologizing to your wife, you need to *mean* it.

Finally, apologize to your wife: acknowledge your mistake, take responsibility, don't make light of it, and don't leave stuff out. Ask if there's anything you can do to make up for it. Put simply, make your apology humble, sincere, and complete.

Don't be afraid to apologize to your wife like a Canadian. She'll appreciate it. Take it further and make it a habit to offer a *good* apology to honor your wife.

Mindset

We all make mistakes. Demonstrate a willingness to acknowledge that simple fact.

Action Item

Examine your conscience. Is there anything you should apologize to your wife about? If so, make a good apology.

Day 22: Forgive Her

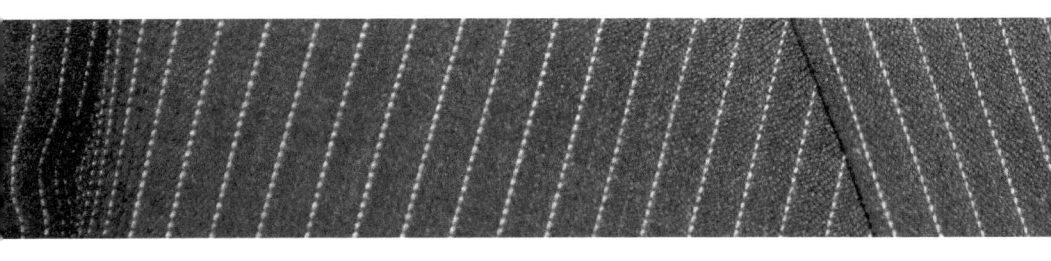

"And forgive us our trespasses, As we forgive those who trespass against us."
— MATTHEW 6:12 —

Now and again, it's at least theoretically possible that your wife will need to ask *you* for forgiveness. This happened to me once, many years ago, in a galaxy far, far away.

No, I'm kidding. My wife occasionally says or does things that are hurtful to me, aided by the fact that I'm sensitive and prone to pouting or self-pity (or both). As a bonus, there's a hot button that tends to send me into an emotional orbit: feeling like someone is taking advantage of me.

These tendencies presented Kathi with a few challenges early in marriage. I tended to brood over various slights, whether of the commission or omission variety. To make things worse, I thrived on verbal affirmation and Kathi wasn't exactly gushy. She's just not a verbal affirmation kind of girl. Occasions for forgiveness abounded.

Thankfully, grace and perseverance have taught us numerous lessons, and we've improved tremendously. One key piece of wisdom has really stuck with me: forgiveness offers an opportunity.

Let me explain.

I've seen breathtaking examples of courageous people who forgive loathsome evil. Among my greatest inspirations is our family friend Rachel Muha, who forgave her son's murderers. Gretchen Crowe beautifully and sensitively wrote her story, *Legacy of Mercy: A True Story of Murder and a Mother's Forgiveness* (Our Sunday Visitor, 2022). Throughout Rachel's story, as throughout human history, forgiveness is an essential element of human thriving. Forgiveness is liberating in at least two ways: spiritual and practical.

In spiritual terms, Jesus made it clear that we are to forgive far beyond our natural inclinations. His admonition to St. Peter to forgive not seven times but seventy times seven times (Matthew 18:22) was shocking then. It's still shocking now.

From a practical standpoint, unforgiveness has been described as "drinking poison and expecting the other person to die." It doesn't work. On the flip side, forgiveness opens up the possibility of healing, including healing the relationship, and frees us from the need for retribution.

So, here's the opportunity. Recall the words of the Lord's Prayer, where we ask that God "forgive us our sins, as we forgive those who trespass against us." I don't know about you, but I would like God to forgive me immediately. When our wives ask for our forgiveness, it's truly an opportunity to grow in holiness and humility by maintaining a spirit of forgiveness and forgiving her right away without holding a grudge.

If you're really ambitious, try forgiving whether your wife asks for it or not. We find the ultimate example of forgiveness in Jesus. Upon being crucified, he cried out, "Father, forgive them; for they know not what they do." (Luke 23:34)

Forgiving like Jesus isn't going to happen spontaneously when you kiss the bride, guys. But your wife, awesome though she is, will provide you with a few chances to grow in this area, and it's *so worth it*. You'll need patience, practice, willingness to communicate, and a dash of humility. Most of all, you'll need God's grace, which is always enough.

Mindset

See forgiveness as an opportunity, and if you need inspiration, think of Rachel Muha.

Action Item

Take some time to think about your wife. Are there any lingering hurts or resentments in your relationship? If so, pray about them and ask for the grace to forgive her completely.

Complement (and Compliment) Her

Then the LORD God said, "It is not good that the man should be alone;
I will make him a helper fit for him."
— GENESIS 2:18 —

Have you ever noticed that good spouses make one another winners, while bad spouses do the opposite? Playing off one another's weaknesses is an attempt at personal gain driven by self-interest. However, playing off one another's strengths is about mutual gain, driven by humility. To see our wives' strengths clearly, we can't be thinking of ourselves.

One of my dad's recurring jokes is about the complementarity of marriage. With a twinkle in his eyes, he says, "God joins you in marriage with the person who will help you grow the most." Then he chuckles.

He's kidding around, but he's not entirely wrong. He and my mom are great examples of truly good spouses. They're still growing, even in their 80s. Their dignity, value, and ability to complement one another remain powerful examples.

My parents and I have a phone call every Sunday afternoon. We often speak more frequently, but it's a cherished time we set aside each week to talk and share life. We've fallen into a familiar pattern. Mom's mobility has deteriorated, so Dad typically has her positioned near the phone in anticipation of my call. When he answers, he puts the phone on speaker, and they immediately want to know how I'm doing. No detail is unimportant, particularly when it comes to Kathi and all the kids and grandkids.

When I ask how they're doing, the standard answer is "boring." I assure them that boring is a good thing since excitement at their age would likely involve a 911 call. They trade compliments and tell me how the other is such a wonderful spouse and how they're still very much in love after more than 60 years of marriage. They express their lack of fear about what they euphemistically call passing through the "big white door" and let me know that when they die, it's okay; they've had extraordinary lives. I ask if they need anything and occasionally purchase some small item for delivery a day or two later. (A service that consistently elicits their amazement and appreciation.)

My parents have modeled incredible complementarity throughout my life, and I have learned so much from them. Like my parents, Kathi and I are completely different. She's practical; I'm conceptual. She nurtures our kids, and I challenge them. She takes care of the family's health care, and I handle the finances. We play to one another's strengths and make up for one another's weaknesses.

Men are gifted with many positive traits, and we can do great things with our lives. Yet we have a few weaknesses, too. For example, I'm a terrible handyman, so we always need to call a professional for home repairs. When it comes to cars, part of my brain still thinks I'm 18. I get grouchy when I'm hungry. I often work and think about finances more than I should. You get the picture.

Part of what makes sacramental marriage amazing is that so much grace is available, including grace that helps our wives love us despite our weaknesses. Does your wife love you despite your foibles? Let's thank our wives for loving us, imperfect as we are.

In the best cases, we face challenges together. At other times, we *are* challenges for one another. Ultimately, we cause one another to grow and become better people. We're a stronger team by playing to our respective strengths.

Next time you notice your wife being a complement, be sure to tell her… give her a *compliment!* With grace, you and your wife will have many good years together and can have confidence in an eternity of joy beyond the big white door.

Mindset

Your wife is among the greatest gifts God has given you for a happy, holy life. Be thankful!

Action Item

Identify just one of your wife's strengths that makes up for one of your weaknesses. Next time you see it in action, thank her and God for the gift she is in your life.

Trust the Sacred Heart

More than that, we rejoice in our sufferings, knowing that suffering produces endurance, and endurance produces character, and character produces hope, and hope does not disappoint us, because God's love has been poured into our hearts through the Holy Spirit that has been given to us.

— ROMANS 5:3-5 —

I felt like an utter failure. Driving down I-71 toward home late at night, I'd just completed a 14-hour day at work. I was in the "partner run" phase of my career, an intense process that proved whether I could cut it as a partner in my CPA firm. At that moment, I couldn't shake the deep conviction that I wasn't spending enough time at work to be successful. I also recognized that I wasn't spending enough time at home to be successful there.

That night, a sorrowful and plaintive prayer spontaneously erupted from my heart. It was an offering of the pain and utter defeat I felt. Something had to give.

The Lord answered my prayer from that night. A few months later, Kathi was pregnant... again. Soon, we discovered the baby had medical challenges. It was a hard time for the entire family and led me to leave my CPA firm. As you might imagine, that didn't solve all our problems. We had never done the math early in our marriage, but when you have a bunch of kids in a short time, you wind up with a bunch of teenagers a few years later. We regularly had two or three at a time, with gusts of up to four.

Teens are terrific, but they have their share of hardships to navigate in that phase of life. Ours were no exception. They (mostly) weren't as bad as their "Preacher's Kid" father, but there were still plenty of stumbling blocks. Their struggles were mostly typical for teens in our broken culture, but a few cases were more serious. Although parenting in the tougher times seemed vaguely penitential, it was also troublesome for Kathi and me in our marriage. There's some truth in the saying that parents are only as happy as their least happy child.

Part of the difficulty was that Kathi and I were raised differently. We had profoundly different viewpoints on how to best handle challenges. She favored a firm hand of guidance, while I preferred giving the teens more freedom to make decisions and enjoy—or suffer—the consequences. We became irritants to one another. Our bickering and disagreements about parenting added to the burden we bore through those years. A negative cycle developed as we argued about the difficulties abounding in our teens. It felt like we couldn't catch a break.

By God's grace, a solution came to our attention.

Friends of our family had learned about the powerful "home enthronement" to the Sacred Heart of Jesus. Devotion to the Sacred Heart began in ancient times and took different forms over the centuries. The practice became widespread in the late 17th Century after Jesus appeared to St. Margaret Mary Alacoque, a French nun, and made twelve promises for those who returned his love.

The enthronement invites Jesus to be the King of our home and family life. And we really need that.

Although prayer and other devotions often change our hearts, circumstances don't automatically conform to what I ask for in prayer. God's not some cosmic vending machine or genie who grants wishes. But in the time following the enthronement of the Sacred Heart, there was a discernible change within our family. It was as if the burdens we carried became lighter, the emotional pressure dissipated, and peace grew in ways we didn't anticipate.

Whether we're facing tough times at work, adolescent-fueled angst, spousal disagreements, or any other problems, the Sacred Heart of Jesus is there for us. Enthroning your home, workplace, parish, or school provides us with the best possible environment for marriages and families to flourish.

Mindset

Faith doesn't make life easier. But it provides the purpose and tools to navigate even the most challenging situations. God can use those situations for our good and his glory.

Action Item

If you haven't already, prayerfully consider enthroning your home to the Sacred Heart of Jesus. If you have done so in the past, renew your enthronement. For more information on this incredible devotion, see www.welcomehisheart.com.

Date Her

As therefore you received Christ Jesus the Lord, so live in him,
rooted and built up in him and established in the faith,
just as you were taught, abounding in thanksgiving.
— COLOSSIANS 2:6-7 —

As I mentioned, Kathi and I married when we were young. In those early years, we often discussed our hopes and dreams for the future. We both had a sense of adventure and talked about the prospect of children, buying a house, places we wanted to visit, and even who we would like to emulate.

More than three decades later, we continue to share our dreams with one another. They're a bit more modest and maybe just a little less idealistic these days. But one thing is consistent: we want to achieve them together. I'm so grateful to have shared life with this incredible woman for so many years, for the family we've built, and for our past and the future time.

Dreaming together is essential. It can also be problematic when life is proceeding at a frenetic pace, and we're being pulled in too many different directions at once. Has that ever happened to you?

It sure has for me. I worked in a large CPA firm for many formative years of my career while my family was expanding. I remember times when Kathi and I were like two ships passing in the night, with me working long hours and Kathi taking the kids to all sorts of activities and events. During that phase of our marriage, it was tough finding time for us to be together, let alone dream together.

It took me years to stumble into the idea that we needed a date night, a time set aside to focus on one another and our marriage. When our kids were young, sometimes it was as simple as bringing in takeout for dinner on Friday nights and letting them watch a movie in the family room. Eventually, we could go out more often and even afford the occasional babysitter.

That time together each week became precious and helped us through the hectic phases of life. One of my colleagues suggested that I prioritize my wife as I would my most important client, and I took the idea to heart. I put date nights with my wife on the calendar and guarded the appointment fiercely. I looked forward to each Friday. In my overburdened schedule, it became one of the most important events, right up there with going to Mass on Sundays.

In retrospect, I wonder whether my overly busy schedule exacerbated our need for a date night. This was a struggle for decades. Not only did I have demanding and time-consuming roles for my "day job," I was also on various boards of directors and then began writing and speaking on top of it all. It took me years, but I finally learned that saying "no" was a critical skill for a happy wife... and life!

Fortunately, my schedule isn't quite as packed these days, and I get to take Kathi out more often. I enjoy it every bit as much as our old Friday date nights, and I hope there are many more years of dates ahead.

Mindset

As the saying goes, our wives spell "love" T-I-M-E. Before marriage, we were willing to invest many hours into our relationships. Remember to keep that going; she's worth it.

Action Item

If you haven't done so recently, ask your wife out on a date. Then ask her about her dreams for the future!

Ease Her Fears

Bear one another's burdens, and so fulfil the law of Christ.
— GALATIANS 6:2 —

I'll never forget my dad's advice when I looked for my first job. "Find the perfect company," he intoned gravely. Then, with a grin, he continued, "Then, when you get there, it won't be perfect anymore."

Gee, thanks.

Dad wasn't highlighting my many imperfections. Rather, he was pointing to a universal truth: Companies aren't perfect because they are made up of people.

Marriages are the same: no marriage is perfect. When Kathi and I were married, we brought all our imperfections into the marriage, along with our joys, sufferings, triumphs, and failures. We also brought our past life experiences, including those from our families of origin, to our present and future.

Experiences impact who we are and who we become. Those involving pain or difficulty, particularly during childhood, may loom large in our human formation. We all know people who have experienced traumatic events such as losing loved ones in tragedies or suffering abuse, neglect, or physical violence. Family dysfunction is alarmingly common in our culture and may result from factors such as substance abuse, poor communication, or lack of empathy.

Often, it's hard to tell someone is bearing a heavy burden. Through executive oversight in my company's human resources department, it dawned on me that many of the company's employees were going through severe hardships at any given time. While that was a clear indicator for the need for greater kindness and compassion in the workplace, it's also true of our spouses. Your wife's past struggles might not be immediately apparent.

Our wives—often through no fault of their own—bring particular wounds into marriage. While most of us aren't trained professionals with years of study under our belts, there is something we can do:

We can help ease her fears.

One of the great gifts of marriage is our ability to impact our wife's life profoundly. Do you know what your wife's greatest fears are? What are the sources of her wounds?

With God's grace, we can help. Part of that help is practical. Does she fear that you'll lose interest in her? Show that interest consistently. Is she worried that you'll abandon her? Stay by her side, always. Love your job more than her? Ensure your commitment to your career doesn't become disordered. Everyone who walks down the marriage aisle has some fear that things won't work out as they had hoped. Recognizing those fears can help us become sensitive to deep and abiding needs within our wives.

We can also recognize our limitations and admit that some wounds require professional or pastoral help. If that's the case, do your best to understand your wife's needs, help her determine the best approach, and provide your support. Especially with highly sensitive and emotionally charged matters, remember to respect her freedom and love her whether things get better or not.

There's something more we can do: we can model ourselves after Christ. Doing so is the best way to love our wives, and, with our cooperation and perseverance, there is the possibility (although not the certainty) that Christ will heal them. The "toolbox" of a Catholic is vast when it comes to the spiritual support of our wives. We must give the Holy Spirit room (and time) to help heal our wife's wounds. Otherwise, we may cause new ones ourselves!

Mindset

Hear your wife's fears and wounds, and support her with patience and love.

Action Item

Next time you inadvertently hit one of your wife's emotional hot buttons, try to gently and patiently understand why it's so important to her.

Communicate With Her

He who goes about as a talebearer reveals secrets,
but he who is trustworthy in spirit keeps a thing hidden.
— PROVERBS 11:13 —

When Kathi and I started having kids, it was a whirlwind. Our first three kids arrived within two years and eight months, resulting in tremendous messiness, sleeplessness, and various forms of chaos. Thankfully, we were young and energetically made it through that phase, although not always with good humor.

Fast-forward a generation. Our middle daughter Maria and her husband managed to beat us. Their first three kids arrived within two years and *six* months. So we have three spirited young grandkids who come from out of town to visit occasionally. Ages five, four, and three, as of this writing (their infant brother doesn't yet accompany them). They're all great kids, but if they stay for a few days, we're exhausted by the time they leave!

Thus, during visits, naps are essential. We sometimes pull a time-honored trick at nap time: we get the teenage auntie (our daughter Hannah) to put them to bed. Of course, Hannah is grouchy since she's been tasked with this thankless chore, so she's in no mood to negotiate with little kids. Except little kids sometimes say the darndest things. Recent example:

> *Grouchy Auntie:* "It's time for your nap. Lie down and go to sleep."
> *Uncooperative Four-Year-Old:* "That's not the way the world works."

Howls of laughter emanated from our family room (that might have been me), followed by exasperated protests from the Grouchy Auntie that, indeed, this is the way the world works along with promises of various negative consequences for non-compliance.

"That's not the way the world works." From the mouth of a four-year-old! It still makes me chuckle to think about it.

It struck me that communication can often be strained between teenage aunts and their non-compliant nieces and nephews. Yet, is this any worse than the communication challenges within a marriage? Especially when you throw in hurdles ranging from everyday irritants (schedule conflicts, fatigue, work pressures) to serious disruptions (illness, job loss, death in the family).

It took Kathi and me a great deal of time and effort to improve our communication. We gradually learned that our words matter. We recognized the importance of setting aside time to focus on one another. We did our best to uphold a basic level of courtesy when we spoke, using words like "please," "thank you," and "you're welcome."

Much ink has been spilt on communication in marriage, and I've read a lot of it in hopes of bettering myself. It's worth learning more about. Remember that all communication isn't verbal. There are lots of other ways we communicate with our wives. However, allow me to offer two very modest suggestions of things you can try.

First, be intentional about discussing some of the most meaningful aspects of your life together on a regular schedule. For Kathi and I, that means weekly; for you and your wife, it could be more or less frequently. We originally discovered this insight when we learned natural family planning, which necessitates speaking about substantive topics regularly. Subsequently, Kathi and I came up with our "five areas" we often discuss: faith, marriage, children, sex, and finances. Our conversations on these topics have little structure, but we revisit them regularly. I encourage you to speak with your wife and develop your own areas.

Second, commit to being discreet with these conversations. You want to be your wife's confidante. Kathi has told me she wants to be able to share her heart with me. That's a gift, gentlemen. Treat it accordingly. If you want to share certain elements of your discussions with others, do it with someone equipped to help and committed to confidentiality such as a priest or counselor. Alternatively, set some ground rules with your wife and stick to them. Be trustworthy with sensitive information, guys. Guard your wife's reputation as well as her heart.

Mindset

With few exceptions, intimate communication belongs within your marriage. Protect those conversations well.

Action Item

Come up with your "five areas" or list of most meaningful topics that matter most to you and your wife. Talk with her about the concept and, if she's game, gently put it into practice.

Let Her Decide

"I can do nothing on my own authority; as I hear, I judge; and my judgment is just, because I seek not my own will but the will of him who sent me."
— JOHN 5:30 —

I met my friend Marc through an organization for Catholic business leaders called Legatus. He has a broad smile and a gregarious personality. We immediately became friends. A man of contradiction, he is a Notre Dame graduate yet roots ardently for *The* Ohio State Buckeyes. I ended up working with Marc for over a decade. A natural CEO, he's an incredibly gifted leader. His superpower?

Decision making.

I'm all about making good decisions. My formative career years were spent in a CPA firm. Advising clients on complex financial matters requires a certain level of precision, particularly when the consequences of that advice have multiple zeroes attached. Accordingly, my decision-making style was deliberate and reflective. You can imagine that when we began working together, Marc's hyper-decisive approach was a positive disruptor of my decision-making style.

Marc can make a thousand decisions in a day. 99.9% are excellent and he's open to changing course on the 0.1%. Much to my amazement, his willingness to make decisions with less-than-perfect information took an enormous amount of work off my shoulders: financial models could be good, but they didn't need to be perfect. We would look at the available data, discuss the strategic implications of decisions, and Marc would decide. Then on to the next problem we needed to solve.

Marc helped me become more decisive. Now and again, I probably caused him to slow down a bit. Melding our different approaches helped us make better decisions.

In many ways, Marc and I have contrasting work styles that reflect a similar pattern at home. Kathi is a practical thinker; I'm more conceptual. She thinks things through by herself in advance of a discussion, while I like to discuss circumstances to ensure I'm not missing anything. She tends to be more tactical and makes decisions on the fly, while I'm slower and more strategic. They're fundamentally different approaches but complementary.

In our marriage, Kathi is exceptionally well equipped to make the thousand and one daily practical decisions required to manage a busy family. She also deals with extremely important matters such as education for the kids and health care for the family. In contrast, I'm more comfortable with financial planning or discerning a life-changing event such as relocation.

Here's the opportunity. Too often, in our culture, decision-making is viewed through the lens of power. Husband and wife are viewed as competitors with different areas of responsibility. That's not right. What we're aiming for is to make the best decisions possible in accordance with God's will. It's not a competition between spouses. It's a question of faithfulness to each other and God. Encourage her to make the decisions that are properly hers to make, and work on more impactful ones together. Why?

Together, you'll make better decisions. Then trust the many decisions your wife makes that don't require your input.

How do we achieve that in practical terms? Part of it is embracing the humility necessary to see your wife's complementary decision-making gifts. These gifts are intended for mutual benefit and are essential to faithful decisions. It's about debating ideas, not your wife, and the two of you discerning the best possible decision together. Recognize when it's okay for one of you to decide. This fulfills our responsibility before God as a couple.

Good decisions in marriage are a team sport. It works for both the Fighting Irish and the Buckeyes!

Mindset

Your wife's decision-making abilities complement yours. It's another way you're better together.

Action Item

Resolve to tackle significant issues with your wife. Make faithful decisions by respectfully asking one another difficult questions, speaking the truth in love, and discerning God's will through prayer.

Day 29:
Help Her When She Hits a Wall

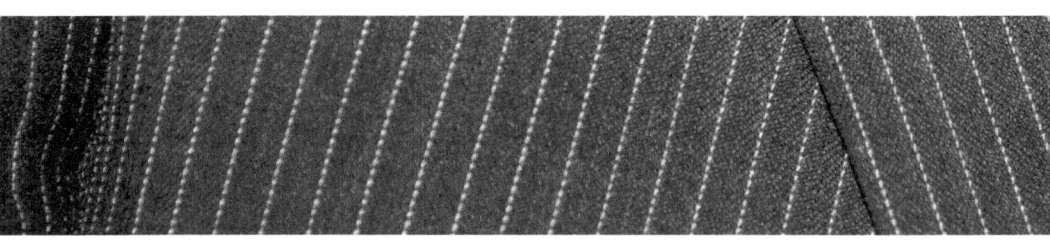

Therefore encourage one another and build one another up, just as you are doing.
— 1 Thessalonians 5:11 —

In my work life, I have often been responsible for executive oversight of human resources. Thankfully, that usually meant competent HR professionals were doing the real work. However, it has also meant that some of the craziest, messiest situations wound up on *my* desk. I sometimes wished for a magic wand that could make it all disappear.

One of the lessons I learned over the years is that, at any given time, many people—more than you would think—are going through challenging situations. Perhaps it's a battle with cancer. The death of a family member. Financial stress. Betrayal. Accident. Divorce. Loss of a job. These types of circumstances are incredibly stressful and emotionally draining.

People often maintain a strong front to hide their woes, so detecting when something is wrong is often impossible. Some people carry even the most serious struggles beneath the surface. While some wear their emotions on their sleeves, others do not. This called for a "high-empathy leadership approach." Treating others with dignity and respect was a baseline, but aiming for even better than that was essential. Namely, treating people with honor and compassion.

So, what does this have to do with honoring our wives?

First, it's a reminder to do what we can in an effort to lessen some of our natural tendencies that can cause us to dishonor our wives. At times, I am not a perfect example of sensitivity. Yes, it's hard to imagine, I know. But seriously, there are times when Kathi needs me to put my empathy into a higher gear. She wants me to recognize her need for emotional support, even if she doesn't say it aloud. That means I'd better be paying attention.

Sadly, I'm not always paying attention. Sometimes, I'm just thinking about myself: my needs, challenges, or whatever I'm after.

During the writing of this book, my wife's grandmother passed away. You may recall I mentioned her earlier. She was 102. She watched her husband be deployed to Europe during World War II as an Army Ranger. She raised a family in the midst of it all. She outlived her husband and all four of their children. A woman of abiding faith, she inspired our entire family. We have pictures of her that include five generations. She knew her great-great-grandchildren.

Kathi held Grandma's hand in her final moments as she slipped away. It was the holy death we had prayed for, and we continue to pray for her soul. But even with Kathi's strong faith, her sense of loss is palpable. Grandma was there for Kathi her entire life.

As husbands, we can't fix every problem our wives will face. Relatives pass away, teenagers have free will, and tragedies sometimes occur. We're not the savior, but we can model Jesus Christ and point to him.

Sometimes, our wives need us to be present and give them a secure place to rest and rejuvenate. Because we know them deeply, we can recognize when their tanks are empty. When they've hit a wall (physical, emotional, spiritual, etc.), they may have nothing to give and need love and care themselves. Hopefully, one way or another, we can support them, pray for them, and model Jesus for them.

Even if you're like me and don't always know what to do at a particular moment, try asking what she needs right now. It's an honest question, and she'll probably appreciate that you asked.

Mindset

Observe your wife when she experiences particularly difficult times. Remember to increase your empathy a couple of notches.

Action Item

Next time you don't know how best to support your wife in a time of need, ask her.

Day 30: Lead Her In Faith

Husbands, love your wives,
as Christ loved the Church and gave himself up for her.
— EPHESIANS 5:25 —

Years ago, I became convinced that the Catholic faith is true. The tipping point happened through sheer grace after I had begun praying the Rosary as a Presbyterian. Weird, I know. Within about three weeks, I wanted nothing more than to become Catholic and receive the Eucharist. My hunger for communion was so intense that I led Kathi and our two infant sons out of Mass each week before the consecration because I couldn't handle not being able to partake.

In a different way, Kathi was also making her way towards the Catholic faith. She says I was flying down an open highway while she hacked her way through dense brush at the side of the road. I was *focused*. On the other hand, Kathi had two babies to care for and was soon expecting a third. Suffice it to say we were traveling the same road at very different speeds.

Around the same time, my parents experienced a similar phenomenon. My dad, a Presbyterian minister, was ahead of my mom on their conversion journey. So imagine my surprise when I visited shortly after Kathi and I entered the Church, only to discover that he was attending Mass six days a week and preaching in the Presbyterian church on Sunday!

My dad's delay was intentional. He believed that the Lord had put him with my mom first and that whatever they did from a faith standpoint, they should do it together. In our conversations, he emphasized the importance of respecting her freedom (the topic of Chapter 14) and removing any pressure or manipulation. There might have been an implicit pull, but certainly no push.

We can't pressure our wives to love and honor us any more than we can pressure them to love and honor God. Conversion isn't genuine if it's coerced, nor is love itself. We could do a fantastic job at every challenge discussed in this book and many others, but that doesn't guarantee our wives will reciprocate. Our wives have free will.

We can't force them, but there is something we *can* do: we can strive for our own faithfulness every step of the way. We can embrace the sacraments and abundant graces that manifest God's infinite love and mercy. We can pray like crazy for ourselves, our wives, and our families. In short, we can be the best possible Catholics we can be. We can live the faith like our lives depend on it, because they do!

When we truly love our wives, we "will the good" for them. We desire what is best for them. Our sacramental marriages provide a means for eternal salvation, which is the greatest good of all.

Someone once told me that when we stand before God, we have no rights, only responsibilities. Think about that for a moment. When we face the God who created the universe, will we have a lifetime behind us of trying to lead our beloved wives to Him? Or will he find that we have failed in that responsibility? None of us is perfect, of course, but we can all resolve to desire her salvation and act accordingly.

The beauty of this approach is that not only does it help propel us along the path of sanctification—along with our wives—it provides a lifetime of joy *right now*. What if your wife needs a bit of evangelization? Within families, but especially within marriages, I believe that the most persuasive witness is our own conversion. She'll notice if we allow ourselves to be truly conformed to Christ. Hand yourself over for her, as Christ did for His Church. As St. Paul says, "I consider that the sufferings of this present time are not worth comparing with the glory that is to be revealed to us." (Romans 8:18)

Mindset

Our faith gives life meaning. It provides countless graces and consolations during our lives and gives purpose to difficult times.

Action Item

Don't pressure her, but share one thing you've discovered about your faith that excites you and invite her to continue growing in her faith.

Persevere With Her

But he who endures to the end will be saved.
— MATTHEW 24:13 —

I'm getting more sentimental with age. My super-cute wife keeps getting cuter in my eyes. The fact that we've been together for so long means that we've grown as individuals and as a couple. It makes me smile when she's kind and understanding with our kids, who are now adults and deal with adult-level challenges. They didn't always show it as teenagers, but they truly appreciate Kathi's affection, advice, and hugs. They genuinely love their mom.

I watch Kathi spend time with our young grandchildren, feeding them, changing them, playing with them, and being completely devoted to their well-being. Her stamina in caring for the grandkids seems limitless, just like their appetites. They love their "Gigi."

Marrying my wife was better than hitting the lottery. Money can be squandered or spent, even in great quantities, but marriage is the gift that keeps giving. Our wives are not perfect. Heck, neither are we.

But like my dad says, God puts us with the person who will help us grow in holiness the most. That means that everything that happens along the way, whether blessings or challenges, can help us grow closer to God and inch our way toward sainthood.

Part of the human condition is enduring difficult situations that arise. Kathi and I have been through tough times, big and small. Career disappointments, illnesses, financial setbacks, the loss of loved ones, relationship problems... none of us is exempt from the trials of life. Some of life's calamities can be downright disorienting, causing us to question everything and even lose hope.

When this happens in marriage, think of this phrase: "The fundamentals are in place." That means God has provided us with the means necessary to overcome whatever challenges we face. The fundamentals include our faith and the great gift of the sacraments, including the Eucharist, confession, and our sacramental marriages.

Even a pile of money from the lottery has limits on what it can do for us in this life. Money can't buy happiness, but marriage prepares us for an eternity of happiness. Next time you spend a moment with your wife, remember how precious she is, and thank her for the treasure she is to you. If you're still sharing time together, these *are* the good old days.

My dad continues to inspire me in this sense. My mom can't take care of him anymore, at least not the way she did for many years. Yet my dad's determination to serve my mom is an inspiration. He cooks (or heats stuff up), cleans (better than a professional, according to my mom), and ties her shoes. Every time I speak with them, they tell me how much they continue to enjoy one another's company and love one another.

My parents know their time together on this earth is not forever. Their lives and marriage have entered a time when the fragility is easier to see. The commitment they made to one another is going to end. They don't know when, but they're running the race to win and persevere to the end.

Or is it to the beginning?

Maybe that big white door isn't the finish line, but rather it's the starting gate to eternity. Looking at it this way, my parents' incredible sacramental marriage is what helped them get there, used by God in ways far beyond what we'll ever know in this life.

And thinking of it that way, that's the purpose of my sacramental marriage too. And yours.

I pray that we'll all be good friends in heaven.

Mindset

Marriage is for life. Ponder that.

Action Item

Pray for the grace of final perseverance for yourself and your wife.

129

Prayers for Marriage

There are countless wonderful prayers for your marriage that you can access online with a quick search, applicable to just about any situation you encounter. There is tremendous depth and beauty in the Church's prayer life, the ultimate prayer being the Mass itself. I encourage you to offer the graces of the Mass regularly for your wife and her intentions.

In addition to the incredible treasury of prayers given to us by the Church, we can always pray from our hearts to the Lord. Remember that there is a special power in prayer that is accompanied by fasting.

It would be easy to fill a book on prayers for marriage (and such books exist), so here are just a few that might be helpful, beginning with the ones that have been particularly meaningful in my own prayer life.

The Rosary

Despite my Presbyterian upbringing, the Rosary helped propel me into the Catholic Church and has become part of the foundation of my prayer life. I can't recommend it highly enough. Prayer for your wife through the Rosary is a huge gift! If you're not familiar with how to pray the Rosary (as I wasn't), here is an excellent guide:

www.usccb.org/how-to-pray-the-rosary

Note that you can also pray the Rosary through various other means, including prayer apps such as Hallow.

The Divine Mercy Chaplet

Here's another prayer that I lean on daily. One of my favorite priests told me that praying the Divine Mercy Chaplet is perhaps the most loving thing you can do for someone. So it makes sense that this prayer is terrific for our wives! Shorter than the Rosary, reciting a chaplet helps us to contemplate the incredible mercy of God. You can pray the chaplet on the Hallow app as well.

www.thedivinemercy.org/message/devotions/pray-the-chaplet

The Memorare

Remember, O most gracious Virgin Mary,
that never was it known that anyone who
fled to thy protection, implored thy help,
or sought thy intercession, was left unaided.

Inspired by this confidence
I fly unto thee, O Virgin of virgins,
my Mother.

To thee do I come, before thee I stand,
sinful and sorrowful.

O Mother of the Word Incarnate,
despise not my petitions,
but in thy mercy hear and answer me.

Amen.

A priest friend calls this the "bazooka of prayers." It's also handy for what some call the "flying novena" which St. Mother Teresa of Calcutta was known to pray for urgent situations. This consists of saying the *Memorare* nine times in a row, rather than over a nine-day period. A tenth *Memorare* is often added in thanksgiving.

Prayer of a Couple on the Anniversary of Marriage

We praise you, O God,
we bless you, Creator of all things,
who in the beginning made man and woman
that they might form a communion of life and love.

We also give you thanks
for graciously blessing our family life
so that it might present an image of Christ's union with the Church.

Therefore, look with kindness upon us today,
and as you have sustained our communion amid joys and struggles,
renew our Marriage covenant each day,
increase our charity, and strengthen in us the bond of peace,
so that we may forever enjoy your blessing.

Through Christ our Lord,

Amen.

This is a wonderful prayer for anniversaries from the USCCB. Celebrating milestones is important, and this prayer can be part of observing a wedding anniversary.

Prayer for a Married Couple

O God, who in creating the human race
willed that man and wife should be one,
keep, we pray, in a bond of inseparable love
those who are united in the covenant of Marriage,
so that, as you make their love fruitful,
they may become, by your grace, witnesses to charity itself.
Through Christ our Lord,

Amen.

Source: USCCB

In Challenging Times

Father, be with our family as we navigate our challenges. Teach us to
trust in your plans and remember your faithfulness. We put our
sufferings and fears, our hopes and dreams, into your hands. Be with
everyone who suffers, especially those who are alone. Make our family,
like the Holy Family, a place of prayer and love—and a refuge for
others who suffer. Mary, help us to ponder, as you did, the meaning of
our experiences, especially when we don't fully understand the
circumstances in our lives.

Amen.

Source: Archdiocese of Detroit

Prayer of St. John Paul II for Families

Lord God, from you every family in Heaven and on earth takes its name. Father, you are love and life. Through your Son, Jesus Christ, born of woman, and through the Holy Spirit, the fountain of divine charity, grant that every family on earth may become for each successive generation a true shrine of life and love.

Grant that Your grace may guide the thoughts and actions of husbands and wives for the good of their families and of all the families in the world.

Grant that the young may find in the family solid support for their human dignity and for their growth in truth and love.

Grant that love, strengthened by the grace of the sacrament of marriage, may prove mightier than all the weaknesses and trials through which our families sometimes pass.

Through the intercession of the Holy Family of Nazareth, grant that the Church may fruitfully carry out her worldwide mission in the family and through the family.

We ask this of You, Who is life, truth and love with the Son and the Holy Spirit.

Amen.

My dad met St. John Paul II many years ago and it was a transformative event in Dad's conversion process. This beautiful prayer written by St. John Paul II for families continues to resonate.

Source: www.mycatholicprayers.com

Intercessory Prayer to St. Raphael for Troubled Marriages

O Glorious St. Raphael, Archangel of healing, intercede for our marriage today. Bring our marriage the same heavenly gifts you brought Tobias and Sarah, the celestial graces of healing, deliverance, and marital unity.

Infuse into our hearts the peace and confidence that nothing is impossible with God concerning the renewal of our marriage. Rekindle in our marriage new forgiveness, new humility, new grace, new peace, new purity, new trust, and new love.

O St. Raphael, one of the seven who stand before the throne of God, intercede to the Merciful Father for the miracle of peace and reconciliation in our marriage, through the infinite merits of Our Lord, Jesus Christ, and the consoling power of the Holy Spirit.

O blessed Raphael, guide us on the pathway of marital peace and unity.

Most loving Archangel of healing, I believe in you, I trust in you, and I thank you.

Amen.

Intercessory prayer is another powerful way to ask for help when we really need it.
This prayer invoking St. Raphael is tremendous.

Source: www.catholicforlife.com

Prayer to Blessed Karl of Austria

O Blessed Emperor Karl, you accepted the difficult tasks and burdensome challenges that God gave you during your life. In every thought, decision and action you trusted always in the Holy Trinity. We pray to you to intercede for us with the Lord our God to give us faith and courage, so that even in the most difficult situations of our earthly lives we may not lose heart, but continue faithfully in the footsteps of Christ. Ask for us the grace that our hearts may be molded into the likeness of the Sacred Heart of Jesus. Help us to work with compassion and strength for the poor and needy, to fight with courage for peace in our homes and in the world, and in every situation to trustingly place our lives in the hands of God, until we reach Him, as you did, through Christ our Lord.

Amen.

IMPRIMATUR: ARCHDIOCESE OF VIENNA, VICAR APOSTOLIC DR. FRANZ SCHUSTER

I ran across Blessed Karl of Austria through a friend of mine who sent me his picture and thought that I was his doppelgänger. As I learned more about his life, his witness of love for his wife and family (eight kids!) really resonated. One quote from the website dedicated to him: "On the eve of their wedding, Karl told Zita: "Now we must help each other attain heaven." He also had a strong devotion to the blessed Mother. This is a wonderful prayer asking for his intercession.

Source: www.emperorcharles.org

Novena to
Saints Louis and Zelie Martin

Another benefit of the communion of saints: asking for the intercession of people who have been married and are now saints. For a particularly powerful novena, look no further than to the parents of St. Therese of Lisieux and her four sisters. Both spouses were canonized together, something we can all aspire to!

www.praymorenovenas.com/saints-louis-and-zelie-martin-novena

For God's Presence

Lord, thank you for dwelling in our very own family,
with all its daily troubles and joys. Thank you that we can come to you
transparently, with our messiness, without hiding behind a mask of
false perfection. Please guide us as we seek to make our home your
dwelling place. Inspire us with signs of thoughtfulness and kindness so
that our family continues to grow in our love for you and one another.

Amen.

We need God's presence throughout our lives. This prayer is concise, humble and heartfelt.

Source: Archdiocese of Detroit

Acknowledgements

I'm grateful to God that this book came together. By grace, it happened at exactly the right time and with the right people. I pray that the Holy Spirit uses it to transform many hearts and create a holy ripple effect within marriages and families.

My wife Kathi, truly my better half, bears singular credit for the existence of this book. I only decided to write it after she read the first few chapters of the manuscript and encouraged me to complete the project. She inspires me to be a better husband and a better man.

My dear friend, the late Fr. Ray Ryland, told me that I did a great job picking my parents Douglas and Margaret Lowry, and I couldn't agree more. They have exemplified the themes in this book over many decades, and I had a front-row seat to watch and learn. Dad, thank you for your amazing example of honoring your wife.

This book was written partly for my five sons: Christian, T.J., Daniel, Joseph and David. I love you all and hope you find it useful. Ditto for my sons in law. My daughter Mia edited the manuscript in detail, relieving me of any notions that I was a moderately decent writer. Thank you. She and my other daughters, Sarah and Hannah, all love their dad, and it makes me happy. I pray each of you are honored by your husband (or future husband, Hannah!)

I'm thankful to many people who contributed to this book in one way or another whether they know it or not: Mike Aquilina, Gary Irvine, Marc Hawk, Michael Hawk, Joe Patrick, Marcus Grodi (the older brother I never had), Fr. John Riccardo, Bishop Kevin Rhoades, Bishop Earl Fernandes, Fr. Dave Pivonka, Rachel Muha, Scott Hahn, Msgr. Frank Lane, Fr. Stash Dailey, Fr. Thomas Blau, Fr. Dave Sizemore, Chris Stefanick, Pat Lencioni, Jim Wahlberg, Marian Schuda, Dan Spencer, David DeWolf, Fr. Mike Schmitz, Jeff Cavins, Chuck Wilson, Emily Jaminet, Matt Schlater, Don Brey, Tim Jakubisin, Randy Hain, Joe Nawrocki, Mike D'Andrea, Mike Hernon, Br. Rex Anthony Norris, Bill Messerly, Dave Orsborne, Dave Jackson, Tom Foos, Joe Hamrock, Mark Landes, Joel Jansen, Todd Wickerham, Grady Campbell, and everyone whose last name is Ryland. Thank you all!

Mike LaMorte at Catholic Treehouse was my partner on this project and does everything well that I do badly or don't want to do at all. Mike made this book a reality. Working with such a talented and faithful friend has been a great joy and a true gift. Thanks Mike!

Finally, I'm thankful to you, dear reader. I appreciate your willingness to become a better husband. May the Lord bless your efforts.

May the God of peace himself sanctify
you wholly; and may your spirit
and soul and body be kept sound
and blameless at the coming of our Lord
Jesus Christ. He who calls you is
faithful, and he will do it.

— 1 Thessalonians 5:23-24 —

OTHER BOOKS BY KEVIN

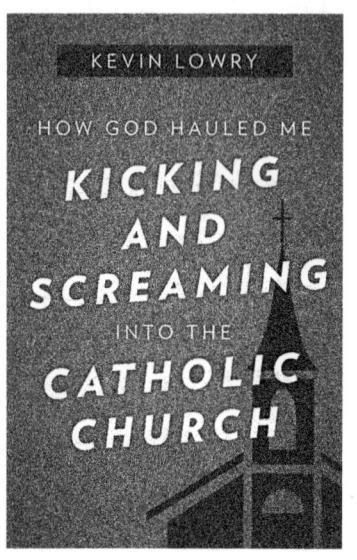

A preacher's kid at a Catholic university, Kevin Lowry settled into a double major in beer and billiards soon followed by uncomfortable run-ins with pious students, failing grades, increasing anxiety, a missing night and the startling realization that some fellow students actually attended Mass the morning after a party instead of sleeping it off.

After getting kicked out, Kevin got his act together, got the MBA, and also got the girl. Meanwhile God was working, drawing him to the inevitable conclusion that Catholicism was all true despite his objections.

Kevin Lowry's journey to Catholicism is fascinating, often funny, and demonstrates God's unfailing, patient love for us all.

How do your motivations, actions, and example at work differ from your motivations, actions, and example at Church?

Explore the benefits of applying the basic tenets of faith—teamwork, perseverance, trust, and goodwill—at work while connecting with the funny and heartfelt lessons learned along the way by Kevin Lowry.

An inspiring exploration of this common and continuous struggle of finding our balance of faith and work.

www.gratefulconvert.com

Enflame your love for the Sacred Heart of Jesus

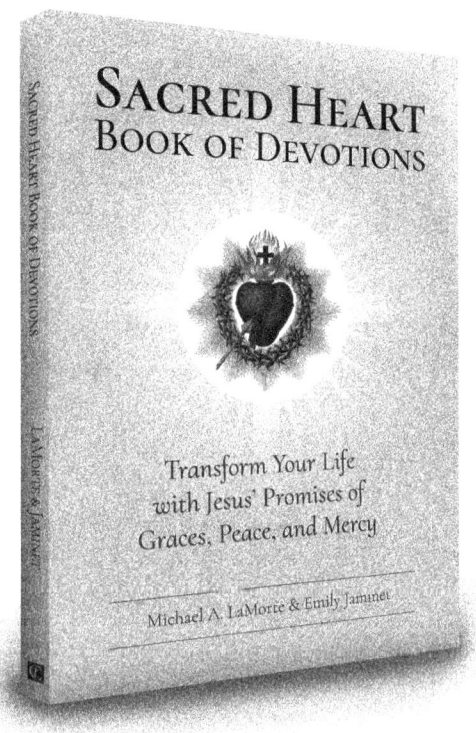

Perhaps the most comprehensive Sacred Heart devotional to date, the *Sacred Heart Book of Devotions* is a timeless collection of essential resources. Full of history, timeless prayers and novenas, classical sacred art, hymns, and more, this is an incredible resource for anyone who has or wants to develop a devotion to the Sacred Heart.

Want to put your faith into action?
Let the saints show you how.

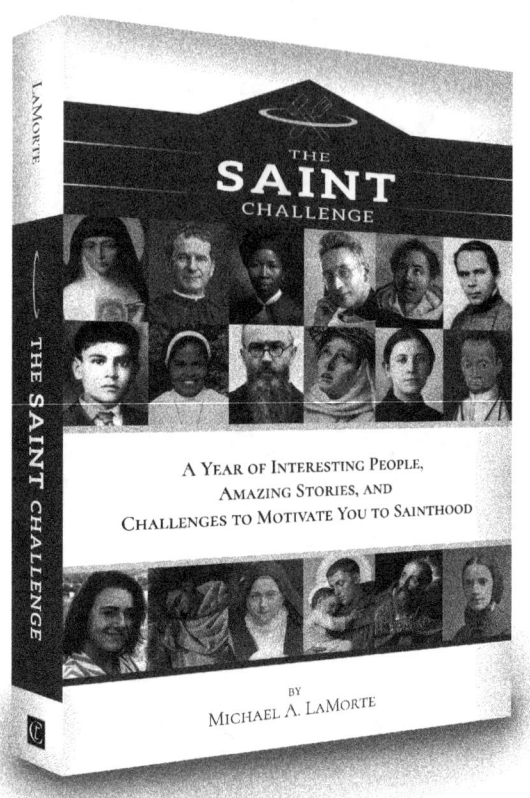

The Saint Challenge is a daily devotional that brings the saints alive and puts your faith to work inspired by their example. Designed to be used over and over, *The Saint Challenge* offers you a unique opportunity to delve into the captivating lives of the saints to find wisdom and inspiration for your own journey of faith. Over 450 pages of stories, challenges, and resources that turn the witness of their lives into inspiration for your personal growth in holiness.

 www.thesaintchallenge.com

www.ingramcontent.com/pod-product-compliance
Lightning Source LLC
Chambersburg PA
CBHW060823120626
46557CB00001B/350